Elijah Kellogg

The Mission of Black Rifle

Elijah Kellogg

The Mission of Black Rifle

ISBN/EAN: 9783744725156

Printed in Europe, USA, Canada, Australia, Japan

Cover: Foto ©ninafisch / pixelio.de

More available books at **www.hansebooks.com**

THE FOREST GLEN SERIES.

THE

MISSION OF BLACK RIFLE;

OR,

ON THE TRAIL

BY

ELIJAH KELLOGG,

AUTHOR OF "ELM ISLAND STORIES," "PLEASANT COVE STORIES,"
"THE WHISPERING PINE SERIES," ETC.

ILLUSTRATED.

BOSTON:
LEE AND SHEPARD, PUBLISHERS.
NEW YORK:
CHARLES T. DILLINGHAM.

PREFACE.

THE story contained in the succeeding pages is one of strong lights and dark shades; and it is thus in virtue of the stormy period during which the events narrated occurred, and because it presents a life-picture of the character and circumstances of men and women who deliberately entered upon a struggle in which life was at stake.

There are wholesome lessons for earnest natures, in the examples of stern endurance, sincere piety, and noble self-sacrifice, with which their history abounds.

With singular ingenuity, stimulated by necessity coupled with a stubborn perseverance, they, while destitute of those appliances considered necessary in older settlements, built mechanical structures in the wilderness, provided schooling and religious instruction for their children, and coolly laid plans in respect to future progress, while experiencing the horrors of an Indian invasion.

The Black Rifle, whose feats were the subject of conversation at the settler's fireside, is no imaginary character, but moved a master spirit among the fierce fighters of those dark and bloody days; and while humanity turns in disgust from the ferocity with which, for wrongs received, he exacted a fearful retribution, we compassionate his woes, and can but admire that matchless sagacity which followed the savage to his haunts, rendered his stratagems useless, and overmatched him at his own weapons. Many a frontier mother laid her babe in the cradle, and turned her spinning-wheel with a lighter heart, after hearing that the Black Rifle had built his camp in the neighborhood.

CONTENTS.

	PAGE
CHAPTER I.	
A RECONSTRUCTED QUAKER	11
CHAPTER II.	
DOMESTIC JOYS	24
CHAPTER III.	
THE FRONTIER SPIRIT RISES	37
CHAPTER IV.	
McCLURE A PEACEMAKER	54
CHAPTER V.	
SHALL WE HAVE THE GIRLS?	64
CHAPTER VI.	
NO SCHOOL, AND PLENTY OF FUN	73
CHAPTER VII.	
HENS ACCUSED OF PREVARICATION	88
CHAPTER VIII.	
THE CHILDREN'S FEAST AND FROLIC	104
CHAPTER IX.	
NAT TAKES A BOLD STEP	118

CONTENTS.

PAGE

CHAPTER X.
THE MEETING IN THE WILDERNESS 142

CHAPTER XI.
INFLUENCE OF THE SCHOOL 162

CHAPTER XII.
A BEAR GOES TO SCHOOL 174

CHAPTER XIII.
THEY RESOLVE TO BUILD A MILL 185

CHAPTER XIV.
PLUCK AND PERSEVERANCE 193

CHAPTER XV.
ROPE-MAKING IN THE WOODS 206

CHAPTER XVI.
HARRY'S PLAN TO GET IRON 215

CHAPTER XVII.
THE LONG-EXPECTED HOUR 226

CHAPTER XVIII.
INDIANS STRUCK WITH PANIC 238

CHAPTER XIX.
THE BLACK RIFLE 254

CHAPTER XX.
ON THE TRAIL 270

CHAPTER XXI.
SURPRISE 282

CHAPTER XXII.
ANGUISH REPLACED BY RAPTURE 300

THE

MISSION OF BLACK RIFLE;

OR,

ON THE TRAIL.

THE MISSION OF BLACK RIFLE;

OR,

ON THE TRAIL.

CHAPTER I.

A RECONSTRUCTED QUAKER.

THE fabric of our dreams is woven, for the most part, either from the circumstances and associations of the previous day, or those of some recent period, while events of a more distant date are not unfrequently mingled with them.

Wrapped in slumber, Bradford Holdness imagined himself still engaged in the various Indian fights and ambushes that had occupied so much of his time and thoughts for the past month.

Just as the light of morning began to penetrate his bedroom, he dreamed that a tomahawk, flung by the hand of a savage, had struck his head; and clapping his hand to his scalp, still excessively sore from the furrow ploughed by an Indian bullet, he leaped upright in bed, and was for the moment quite astonished to find himself in bed, and his wife quietly sleeping beside him.

His attention was now arrested by a thin white streak, that, beginning at a chink between the logs of the house, reached nearly across the floor; and, shoving back the shutter, he found that the stockade and the walls of the blockhouses were plastered, and the ground to the depth of several inches was covered with snow that was still falling.

"Halloa! who's on guard?"

"Harry Sumerford."

"What time did it begin to snow, Harry?"

"I relieved Stewart. He said it begun ter snow 'twixt one and two o'clock."

"Good! now we kin kill the hogs, git well of our hurts, and haul up a good lot of wood in peace. I only hope the snow will keep comin': 'twill stop the trampin' of these redskins while it stays."

When the ground was covered with snow, the settlers were generally free from apprehension of attacks from Indians, as the latter could no longer conceal their tracks, and were afraid to venture. It also relieved them from the fatigue of daily scouting and from very much of the usual guard-duty.

Our readers will therefore sympathize with the frontiersman, as after feasting his eyes upon the falling flakes he closed the bullet-proof shutter, replaced upon his crown the poultice that had become deranged during the night, retired again to his bed, drew the bearskin over him, and, with a grunt expressive of intense satisfaction, was asleep in a moment.

We have been so long in the habit of familiar intercourse with many of our constant readers, as to have quite forgotten that there may be others, who chancing to take up this story might ask, Who is Bradford Holdness? and where is the place said to be his home ? The place referred to, and familiarly known as Wolf Run, is a frontier settlement and disputed territory, claimed both by the Province of Pennsylvania and the Indians, and far in advance of all other settlements, those to the westward having been broken up by the Indians.

The settlers were many of them old hunters, and men born on the frontiers, and bred to Indian warfare. Others of them were Scotch, English, Germans, and men from New England.

They were now in garrison, having been compelled to abandon their farms for the reason that the Indian war, that broke out after the defeat of General Braddock, left the frontier exposed. Here they had collected their families, household goods, and cattle, the greater portion of their grain, hay, and hogs that were numerous.

Late in the fall they had made the astounding discovery that the stock of salt belonging to the community, which was their sole reliance for preserving meat to sustain them through the winter and in the event of a siege, had been dissolved on account of a leak in the roof of the block-house.

They made this discovery at a time when the country between them and the sources of supply was swarming with savages, who flushed with recent victory, strong in numbers, and supplied with arms and ammunition by the French, were slaking their thirst for blood by the massacre of all who fell into their hands.

The settlers found themselves shut up to one or the other of these courses, — either to run the gauntlet of the Indians in order to procure their salt by bringing it on the backs of mules and horses, or to starve where they were.

Men of their stamp were not long in resolving upon the former alternative; but it was a much more difficult matter to select the persons to go upon this desperate errand, and those who were to remain.

They were dealing with an enemy more subtle than the serpent; and it was by no means improbable that the Indians might penetrate their designs, and, during the absence of its defenders, attack the block-house, capture and butcher their families, or with a superior force ambush and surround the salt-carriers, and then lay siege to the garrison.

After long and anxious deliberation they chose a majority of the best men, and boys verging upon manhood, but little inferior to the greater portion of their elders, to go out with Holdness for leader, leaving for defenders several experienced men and the greater portion of the older boys, together with a number of lads from twelve years old and upwards, who by incessant practice were able to shoot well from loop-holes, although obliged to stand on blocks to increase their stature.

They left in command of this home force Edward Honeywood, the best rifle-shot on the frontiers in general estimation, though some considered the Black Rifle a trifle better; but the matter had never been tested. In order to offset taking so large a number of the older boys, they left Harry Sumerford, the superior of them all, and their leader, of whom Holdness was wont to say, that, if there was any milk and water about Harry Sumerford, it took sharper eyes than his to see it; and, if he lived to see three and twenty, there wouldn't be a man 'twixt Raystown Branch and Susquehanna who could lay him on his back at a ring-wrestle, take the heart of a tree away from him, put a bullet nearer the mark, or come up with him for follering a blind trail in the woods. These were the qualifications then most prized, because life depended upon them. "All that a man hath, will he give for his life;" but Harry will develop higher qualities by and by.

When this perplexing matter was settled, the party took up their line of march, not, however, without many a misgiving, trusting rather to the strength of the fortress than to the numbers of the garrison; and more than one of those iron-sided men dashed the tear from his eye as, before burying himself in the woods, he turned to take a last look at the walls which sheltered all he held most dear on earth.

Here they are, my young friends, on the morning after their return, having lost but one of their number, though several are wounded, and all more or less worn down with fatigue.

In consequence of the loss of mules by Indian bullets, they were compelled to bring a portion of the salt upon their backs.

In their company is a boy, Will Redmond, rescued from the Indians with whom they had a battle on the road; likewise an Indian trader, Simon Lombard, also rescued from the same band; and Nat Cuthbert, an old acquaintance whom they met in Lancaster.

"Bradford," said Mrs. Holdness at the bedroom door, "breakfast's ready, but I think you'd better keep quiet: you're wounded and all worn out."

"Not a bit of it. Did you ever hear me say I was tired, all these years we have lived together?"

"Can't say I ever did."

"Well, I never was but once."

"Indeed! when was that?"

"When I was about nineteen; eat so much hulled corn, made my jaws ache. Are the rest on 'em up?"

"They're getting up."

"How good you look, wife! I thought, one spell, 'twas mighty unsartin whether we ever saw one another agin."

"Oh, you don't know, husband, what a bitter lonesome night that first night after you went away was to us here! We women-folks got together, and had a good cry: we started at every little noise, thinking Indians were coming. Mr. Honeywood and the other men-folks had all they could do to encourage us."

"I see how that was; but it's all over for this bout. The snow is falling; and we needn't consarn ourselves about Indians while that lasts. The loss of poor Mugford is all the drawback, but then we got Nat back agin; and that, as far's strength's consarned, makes up for the loss."

"Oh, husband! that won't make up the loss to his wife and children."

"Sartin; but then it's better for them and her, in time ter come, ter have another man step right inter his tracks ter defend 'em; and Cuthbert is wuth more for fightin' than Mugford ever was, if he did come of the Quakers that I despise above ground."

Slowly one after another of the returned party made their appearance, one with a broken arm, Holdness wounded in the head, Ned Armstrong minus a finger, and another limping with a wound in his thigh, and others wounded in various ways. Let us take a look at them, as they are seated at the breakfast-table.

About a third of the way from one end of the board sat Mrs. Holdness, every feature of her fine motherly face manifesting the happiness she felt in having her husband and son once more at home. At her left, and as close as he could squat, was Will Redmond, whom Mrs. Holdness had adopted the moment she saw him. The little fellow bore an ugly scar on his forehead at the roots of the hair, the result of a blow from an Indian tomahawk. Indeed, the boy would have been killed with his parents, had not another savage, who claimed Will as his captive, interfered in his behalf, and prevented his assailant from inflicting a mortal wound. Next to Will sat Prudence Holdness, with the form and features of her mother, but inheriting the high spirit, resolute temper, and strong prejudices of Holdness.

Beside Holdness is his son Cal, and near to him a tall, finely proportioned young man, his left arm in a sling. This is Nat Cuthbert, Quaker born and bred. Ephraim Cuthbert, the father of Nat, was formerly an inhabitant of the Run, and still owned property there.

When at the beginning of the war the settlers resolved to fight the matter to the bitter end, and if need be die for the ground, Nat manifested such entire sympathy with the rest, that his parents, who were Quakers of the " straitest sect," removed from the place to prevent if possible their children from embracing outright the sentiments of the " world's people." In regard to the younger children the effort was successful; but, in the case of Nat, other influences had attained such ascendancy as to defy the remedy.

Notwithstanding, as became a dutiful son, Nat went with the family to a Quaker community in the bosom of the older settlements, where he remained discharging his duty to his parents till of age. He then left home, and, while seeking for employment at Lancaster, lighted upon Holdness and his old neighbors and playmates, who received him with open arms; Holdness, in the true spirit of frontier hospitality, offering him a home in his household.

The invitation was no sooner given than accepted. Arming himself, Nat joined the party, and was wounded on the way in a fight with Indians. How much any lurking affection for Prudence Holdness had to do with the strong desire manifested by Nat to return with the Wolf Run boys, we shall not take upon us to determine; and we are still less capable of divining the effect his return produced on her mind. No wonder she manifested considerable confusion: it was so unexpected.

Between Cuthbert and George Holdness, who fell at the defeat of Braddock, there had existed the strongest friendship; and the love the parents cherished for the dead was in a measure transferred to his dearest friend and companion.

But, however much disposed to regard Nat favorably as an old friend and playmate of George, it is very probable that the Quaker principle of non-resistance would have afforded an effectual barrier to any more tender feeling on the lady's part.

But it was altogether another matter, when instead of the broad-brim, Quaker garb and dialect, Nat Cuthbert presented himself, his well-knit and finely proportioned form arrayed in a hunting-shirt, knife and tomahawk at his belt, and his arm in a sling.

The flush on her cheek was deepened; and the young man thought there was an expression in her eyes he never had seen there before, when McClure, laying a hand on his shoulder, said that he was as cool under fire as an old veteran, and that it was a real godsend to have such a strapping young fellow come among them at such a time as this. Nat, having the use of his right arm, could feed himself, but was unable to cut his food; and, matters being as we have stated, it was not at all singular that Prudence thought it necessary to assist her brother Cal somewhat in cutting the meat and spreading the bread of the wounded youth, and that the latter made not the least objection, though the rest had long ago left the breakfast-table.

"Harry, Harry Sumerford," said Nat as they rose from the table, "what's become of my rifle, powder-horn, and shot-pouch I left with you?"

Harry in a few moments brought them forward, and held up the rifle while Nat examined it, opened and shut the lock with his well hand, put the ramrod in the barrel, and blew in the muzzle. "She's clean as a whistle, Harry, and in first-rate order. You don't know how natural she looks, just like an old friend. What good times I've had with her! How I wish my arm was well, I should so like to try her!"

"Do you remember the time you staid all night with me, and a bear was running off with a pig? You fired, and killed the pig, and I killed the bear, both of us barefooted and bareheaded, just as we jumped out of bed; and we had a bear and a pig both to dress next morning."

"Yes indeed: we were always sure, when we got together, to have something turn up, or to turn something up."

CHAPTER II.

DOMESTIC JOYS.

THE days were now short: the snow had not quite ceased falling.

Those members of the return party who were not wounded were stiff and sore from fatigue; the stones had cut their moccasons, bringing their feet to the ground; and the straps of the packs filled with salt had worn the skin from their shoulders.

There was no work pressing to be done; and it was decided to give the children a holiday from school, and, as they were so abundantly supplied with poultry, to indulge in an extra dinner in honor of their safe return, and the snow-storm to them so great a blessing.

In order that the cattle might have just cause for rejoicing, it was thought best to give them a little salt of which they had long been deprived.

This article though craved by them, and necessary in order to promote their health and growth, was too valuable to be thus used, save in small quantities and at long intervals. The wounds of the injured men were first attended to, Holdness bringing forward a pack taken from the savages,— which contained salves made from herbs and roots known only to them, mixed with bear's fat, and dried barks and herbs scraped and pounded fine for poultices,— and applied them without delay.

"There's no doctor kin go ahead of an Indian for healing wounds," said Holdness, "and making all kinds of salves and poultices."

The next pack that was opened contained the school-books and paper that Mrs. Raymond had sent to the children. Israel Blanchard, taking from his breast-pocket a book, cried,—

"Come here, Eddie Honeywood, and see what your grandfather has brought you."

The little boy took the book, and instantly exclaimed,—

"What's that in it, grandpa?"

Blanchard opened the book; and a bullet dropped out from it, and rolled along the floor.

"You must take good care of that book, Ned;

for it saved your grandfather's life: 'twas in the breast of my hunting-shirt, and stopped the Indian's bullet."

Several other small articles, needles, and matters of that kind, the return party had brought, the value of which to the settlers it would be difficult for us to estimate, who have never known the want of them.

But the general interest attained its height when a pair of saddlebags were opened, in the pockets of which were horse-shoes, horse-nails, a large number of files, awls for making moccasons, several short bars of iron and steel, powder, lead, and gun-flints.

"Oh, the files and the iron!" cried Honeywood, who knew right well how to work it. "Oh, the powder and lead!" shouted Harry Sumerford; but when the guns — some smooth-bores, but the greater part rifles that had been taken from the Indians — were brought in, his joy was unbounded.

"Lombard!" exclaimed Israel Blanchard, "now's your time: afore the women and girls go to cooking, bring out all your stuff, and they'll help you put it to rights."

Simon Lombard, as many of our readers know,

was an Indian trader who, going to Raystown Fort, had on an evil day fallen in with a war-party of Shawanees, who instantly seized him and his goods, which were suited to the Indian trade, including whiskey. He had also several military coats, which, after his visit at Raystown, he had engaged to deliver to Col. Innes at Fort Cumberland; and articles of female apparel that he expected to find sale for among the families of whites who resorted to the fort for safety.

The Indians partook freely of the whiskey, and, coming to a farm that was abandoned, set the buildings on fire as night came on, and made preparations for a grand dance by firelight.

They arrayed themselves and their captive for the occasion. Having stripped the poor wretch, they painted him, put on him a scarlet breech-cloth, tied beads round his neck, stuck his hair full of combs, and, a savage seizing each hand, they would have him to dance with them, every now and then stopping, and putting a looking-glass into his hand, in order that he might admire himself. It is needless to say that all this finery was taken from his own stock of goods, the savages arraying themselves in the uniform suits and scarlet blankets, and each one making sure of beads and a looking-glass.

They were having a glorious time when the light of the flames and the yells of the dancers attracted the attention of Holdness and his men, returning with the salt, who, creeping up while the savages were intent upon their amusement, opened a deadly fire at short range, and then, rushing on with tomahawks, killed the greater part of them, rescuing the trader more dead than alive.

Even at this time he was far from good looking. The paint with which the Indians had daubed him was not entirely removed, and the bear's grease still clung to his hair.

There was a deep cut across his cheek, made by the pieces of broken looking-glass; and it was with difficulty, and only by using the utmost care, that he could sit down, seeing he had been pricked as full of holes as a pincushion, by a savage delegated to bring up his rear with a steel-pointed arrow when he did not keep time with his partners.

After the flight of the Indians, the boys picked up his goods, which were scattered in admirable confusion over the ground, and trodden into it by the feet both of the savages and mules; stripped the garments, ribbons, beads, and uniforms from the dead bodies, and thrust them into the saddle-bags that were now brought in, and their contents laid on the long table and floor.

The men and boys, under the superintendence of the trader, now began to sort out the various articles; and the women and girls prepared water and flat-irons at the great fireplace, to endeavor to cleanse those that were soiled, in order that the owner might be able to dispose of them at a reduced value.

"Isn't that too bad?" said Mrs. Grant, holding up an officer's uniform coat with two bullet-holes through it, covered with blood, and spotted with grease and Indian paint.

"Bad enough," replied Lombard, "but not so bad for me as some other things that are spoiled; for I didn't own the coat. I was only carrying it, and ain't accountable for what the Indians have done."

"Only look here, mother," said Maud Stewart, holding up her apron full of broken combs and damaged Jews'-harps.

"Here's something worse 'n that," cried Dan Mugford, unrolling a blanket in which was a great ball of wet clay full of needles, awls, and Indian beads, mixed with the dirt, and rusted; some broken, some whole, and all stuck together with mud and rust, so that it rolled along like a stone.

"Isn't that too bad? all those nice needles, when there's only one single darning-needle in this Run, Mrs. Israel Blanchard's, and that has gone the rounds till it's almost worn out."

The Indians, in their haste to get at some bottles of whiskey that were stowed in the bottom of the bags, had pulled out the strings of beads and papers of needles, flung them on the ground, and trampled them in the mud. The boys, on the other hand, anxious to lose none, had scraped up mud and all, and tied the whole in a blanket. Along with the needles and beads were several costly sashes that belonged to Lombard. Sashes were universally worn by officers in that day, not merely for ornament, but for another reason. There were no ambulances then; and a sash was of great use in carrying a wounded officer from the field. Those the Indians had tied around their naked waists; and they were soiled with paint and perspiration, two of them with blood, and one was pierced through the different folds by a rifle-bullet.

There is nothing that affords greater pleasure to a savage than to view himself in a looking-glass when painted for war; and it also enables him to lay on the colors himself. Of these in paper frames and of diminutive size, Simon had brought with him a large stock. A few of them had been carried off by the Indians who had escaped, and of the remainder there was not one entire; but the boys, upon the principle of saving the fragments, had collected the broken pieces and frames.

"Oh, what a sin and crying shame!" exclaimed Mrs. McClure, holding up in one hand a bonnet crushed flat as a pancake, and in the other a tangled mass of blue, green, and red ribbons, tied in knots, twisted into strings, the edges torn, and covered with mud.

"If you call that a crying shame, what do you call this?" said Prudence Holdness, pointing to a quantity of scarlet blankets, colored handkerchiefs, and red breech-cloths, that Harry and Ned Armstrong were overhauling.

Among the trader's stock were Indian paints (lampblack and vermilion). The Indians had flung the cloths in a heap, and the papers of paint on the pile. One of the mules, trying to free itself from the saddle, lay down and rolled on the heap, breaking the papers of lampblack, and smearing with it all the blankets that lay on top. This was not all. A hungry mule will eat any thing: they will eat each others' tails and manes off; and one of them, after cropping all the grass within the length of his halter, began to pull the cloths from the heap, and chew them up, and trample them under his fore feet.

Until now Lombard had managed to contain himself; but this was too much. He flung down the ribbons that with shaking hands he was disentangling, tore his hair, cursed in Delaware, French, and English, and seemed like a man demented.

His new friends did all in their power to console him; but he refused to be comforted, and kept on exclaiming, —

"If they'd burnt 'em all up so that I never should have set eyes on 'em agin, I could have stood it; but to see them 'ere nice cloths that cost me so much, and that there's always a profit on, chewed up by a mule, black as a coal, and trampled in the mud, it's too much for flesh and blood."

As is often the case, the appearance was worse than the reality. But a small portion of the articles were entirely worthless. So many ingenious women, willing men, and children, soon gave a different complexion to affairs.

The children sorted the needles and awls, and scoured off the rust with ashes. The ribbons and sashes were washed, scraped with wooden knives, stretched to dry, and then pressed smooth with flat-irons. As to the blankets with which the mule made free, the beast, not finding them very palatable, had only chewed and slobbered, not ground them between his teeth, and being smooth shod had not cut any holes in them with his shoes; and when washed and ironed they appeared little the worse. Even those smeared with lampblack were not spoiled: the texture was not injured; and, as the Indians had not worn them, they were free from grease and blood. These were shaken, brushed with little brooms made of twigs, beaten with rods, and then washed. In short, so much was done in this one day to improve the appearance of his goods, that the trader's spirits rose;

and he sat down to supper quite cheerful, and disposed to be sociable.

"What possessed you to start out on a trading-vige, when you knew the Indians were in arms?" said Grant while they were eating.

"Well, I was kalkerlatin' to call at Raystown, leave part of my truck there, and then go among the Mohawks, 'cause they're neutral. I didn't think I'd meet any Delawares or Shawanees, 'cause I heard they'd gone another way; and if I did I didn't think they'd harm me. They don't often meddle with traders, 'cause they need 'em, and it wouldn't pay: the traders wouldn't come if they did."

"It seems they were ready enough to harm you, and came nigh killing you."

"It was the whiskey. It works different on an Indian from what it does on a white man: it makes 'em ravin' mad. Do you 'spose a band of Indians on the war-path would have made sich a fire as that was, gone to dancin' round it, and yellin' so they could be heard two miles, if they'd been themselves? or do you think as many as there was of you could have crept within near rifle-shot of 'em right in a clear field?"

"No, a snake couldn't have done it. But what made you let 'em know you had whiskey? you might have known what would come of it if you sold it to 'em."

"Think I'm such a fool as that? It came this way. That big mule with a cropped mane was lame in the off fore-leg. I was kinder worried, feared the beast 'd give out 'fore I got to Raystown; and, when I stopped at noon to feed, I gin the whole leg and shoulder a raal soakin' and rubbin' down with whiskey, and they smelt it."

"Ay; they'd 'a' smelt it if 't had been a week old. You was short-sighted there."

"What could I do? The beast was like to fall lame. If it hadn't been for that, they wouldn't have hurt nor robbed me; I'd 'a' given 'em a little powder and a few bullets, and they would 'a' let me alone. I wasn't kalkerlatin' to take liquor into the Indians' country, only to the fort where I'd been safe in sellin' it, and where 'twould have brought a great price 'mong the officers, soldiers, and friendly Indians what come there to trade furs. A bottle of rum when an Indian's hankerin' arter it 'll buy more furs than a whole mule-load of lookin' glasses, beads, and sich like; but, if I'm goin' to sell it to 'em, I want to do it through a loophole, and stand inside."

After supper great logs were piled on the andirons; the night was quite cold, and they drew in a large circle around the fire for a social chat.

There was no lack of subjects for conversation. Lombard narrated some of his hair-breadth escapes among the different tribes of Indians, and said that many times, after such experiences, he had resolved that he'd never adventure among them agin, but had always forgotten them resolutions.

Holdness then related some of the circumstances of their expedition to Baltimore and back; and Honeywood gave some account of an attack that had been made by the Indians upon the garrison during the absence of Holdness and his companions.

CHAPTER III.

THE FRONTIER SPIRIT RISES.

THERE was now a brief pause in the conversation, during which Tony Stewart, getting up from his seat in the chimney-corner, whispered somewhat to his mother, who only shook her head. With downcast looks the lad returned to his block in the corner, but after a little crossed the circle to the chair of Proctor, with whom he held conversation in whispers. It was not long before the former said, —

"Mr. Holdness, Honeywood forgot to tell you what the Screeching Catamounts did while you and the rest were absent."

"Ay, indeed: what was it?"

We would inform the casual reader that this terrible appellation belonged to the boys twelve years of age and upwards, who, catching the spirit that animated their elders, had formed themselves into a company with this sounding designation, and whom the exigency had induced their parents to make use of in defence of the garrison.

"You see," continued Proctor, "after you'd gone, we found we had a good many more loop-holes than men to man them; plenty of guns and ammunition, and not enough to use the muskets. We thought as these little chaps were full of grit, and not stout enough to hold out a gun, we'd practise 'em at shooting from a rest, and, when one of 'em got so he could hit fairly, give him a loophole of his own."

"That was a first-rate plan."

"It turned out to be; for, though we had to stick 'em up on blocks to make 'em tall enough to reach the loop-holes, when the Indians attacked us Tony Stewart shot one."

"Shot him ter death?"

"Dead as a hammer."

"Come here, my lad."

Tony with a flushed cheek obeyed.

"You're a brave boy," patting him on the head. "That's more'n I could do at your age; there's not another boy in the land's got sich a record."

The Young Defenders. Page 38.

"Father said he'd buy me a rifle when I got bigger."

"If he don't, I will."

"Johnny Crawford got hit in the leg, and Bobby Holt on his arm; and they didn't nary one of 'em cry a bit, but went back to their loopholes after it was bound up."

"Come here, Johnny; come, Bobby: I want ter look at you, and I want everybody in the room to take notice of you. It will be told of all over the frontier."

"It's a good thing," said McClure, "to have these boys (children, I may say) growing up to the rifle, and getting ready to fill the places of those who are dead and gone; for we've had sore losses, and those we could ill spare, these last few months."

"It's my mind," said Holt, "that we should have had a much longer and sharper siege; but the Indians, meeting so heavy a fire, thought the garrison was full of men, and got discouraged. It isn't every day that boys of thirteen have scars of wounds got in battle to show and be proud of."

"Ned Honeywood," said Holdness (Honeywood was his son-in-law), "why didn't you give the boys the credit of what they'd done, that we all might know it, and praise 'em for it as they deserve?"

"I did praise them after the affair was over, and thought that would do."

"Ah, Ned, you've too many of those old Quaker notions you got when a boy sticking ter you. If you want to put the right fighting grit into boys, you must praise 'em for it as they deserve, rub their ears, and set 'em on jest as the old wolves do their young ones. That's the kind of pluck for the frontier, and it's all the sort 'll answer."

"That's the talk," said Blanchard: "we're just shut up to this. We shall have what we fight for, and nothing else."

"Even sae: that is the gaet we guide the bairns at hame. We gie 'em a sma' stick to practise wi', then a bigger one, and sae till they grow up to the braidsword; praise 'em when they do weel, and sing songs anent the auld chieftains that were sae brave lang syne," said Stewart.

"I am neither Quaker born nor bred; but I have received much kindness from Quakers, and shall always respect and love them. I don't know that they've taught me any thing I need be ashamed of, or that I have any notions which prevent me from defending my life and property and that of my neighbors. I can shoot an Indian, or tomahawk him, if I see good reason; but I won't kill him because he's an *Indian*, neither will I take his scalp. I don't believe courage consists in bloodthirstiness, neither do I want my children to be wolves, and I don't mean to go to the wolves for instruction. It seems to me they are sufficiently inclined that way, without any special painstaking."

"It does my soul good to hear such talk as that," said Mrs. Sumerford. "As you all know, I've got four boys, and they are good boys, too, as ever a poor woman left as I am had to be thankful for; and it used to make me feel so bad to hear them talk — even to those little tots Sammy and Enoch — about nothing else but killing and scalping all the time. When they got up, when they came to the table, and even after they went to bed, I could hear them. That time the Indians waylaid them in the grain, and they shot the Indians, and Enoch and the rest came in with the bloody scalps at their belts, — oh, I shall never forget that! There was Harry didn't want to do a stroke of work on the place, only to range the woods, and talk about killing Indians. As Mr. Honeywood says, they were just like wolves. There I was, neighbors, as you all know, a poor heart-broken woman, — my husband killed, left with all these boys and a piece of land, no dependence in this world but just upon these boys to work it, and they wild harum-scarums, Harry and Elick living in the woods, and longing to turn rangers and Indian-killers, and the little children painting themselves like savages, and flourishing their wooden tomahawks. Oh, it used to make me heart-sick! But, since Mr. Honeywood took Harry in hand, it's put better thoughts in his head. Never mother had a better or more industrious boy; and the others copy after Harry. Then Mr. Honeywood was the means of building a schoolhouse, and setting the school a-going. Now, in the evenings, the boys take their books, and sit down. You couldn't get one of my boys, nor Cal Holdness, nor Ned Armstrong, to take a scalp now."

"It was a mighty good thing for you, Mrs. Sumerford, that your boys had a little of the wolf about 'em, and perhaps for some others, and that

Harry had been brought up to range the woods, and shoot to a hair's breadth, and follow a trail; or your scalp and theirs would now be drying in an Indian wigwam."

"I'm sure, Mr. Blanchard, I would not be ungrateful to them, and especially to a higher Power, for our preservation; but I don't see, and I don't think anybody will say, that Harry or the other boys are not just as ready, when there's danger, to do their part as they were before."

"None of us will dispute that, Mrs. Sumerford; for there are not four better boys on the frontier."

"Perhaps I'm taking too much upon me, a woman, talking so before the men-folks, who know so much more about it than I do."

"Not a bit of it, Mrs. Sumerford," said Holdness: "say every word you have a mind to."

"Perhaps I'm foolish or consated, but it seems to me I know more about the boys, big and little, the way they feel, and their ways, than most of the neighbors, because they've always been in the habit of making headquarters at our house (I s'pose it's 'cause I've so many boys of my own); and there they'll lay all their plans and projects, talk over all their concerns, and tell their thoughts to one another right afore me: they never seemed to mind me one mite.

"Now, I know it can't be said truly that any thing Mr. Honeywood says or does to keep the young people from being bloodthirsty, and, as he says, just like the Indians, goes to hurt their courage, and make them less capable in a bad time; because when my Harry, Ned Armstrong, and Cal, and poor George Holdness who is in a bloody grave, felt that they were old enough, and ought to take their share of scouting, and form themselves into a company, and talked it all over before my fire, they went right to Mr. Honeywood to get his opinion; and he encouraged and advised them, sent them to Mr. Holdness, and talked with the neighbors about it. Upon that, all the children must needs have their company with their wooden guns and tomahawks; and when the greater part of the men-folks went after the salt, and Mr. Honeywood had charge, everybody knows that it was his proposal to learn my Sammy and Tony here, and all the rest of 'em, that couldn't hold out a gun to save 'em, to fire from a rest, and then put 'em into the loop-holes."

"I s'pose," said Holdness, "that McClure, myself, Grant, Armstrong, and some of the rest of us old frontier's men, are a rough set; but we're the kind to git along with these red imps that are all round us jest like the wolves licking their jaws round a sheepfold. If they could git inter this garrison, they'd kill and scalp, or put to the torture over a slow fire, every man, woman, and child, — yes, that little babe that Jean Stewart is now nursing at her breast, and that other little dear of Sally Holt's asleep there in the cradle; and I mean to give 'em as good as they send as long as I kin pull a trigger, or handle a hatchet. I don't reckon on any marcy from them; and they'll git none from me, I promise you. I hate 'em! They've killed and put to the stake the greatest part of my blood-relations, and killed before my eyes two of the best boys ever a father had; and I mean to train up my children to do the same.

"When anybody's living among thieves and robbers, and they've got a young dog that shows there's good grit in him, they give him bloody meat to bring out the savage temper, and make him hard bitten; and that's the way to do with boys fixed as we are, where it's kill or be killed.

It's no place on the frontier for white-livered consarns and meek people that can't strike back."

" Oh, husband, don't talk so!" said his wife. "I'm sure I don't feel so, though I've had many a heart-ache on account of Indians."

" That's just the kind of talk," said Israel Blanchard. " Most of your people here who've always lived in Pennsylvania never have found out till since Braddock's defeat what an Indian is made of; but, if you'd been born and bred where I was, you'd taken it the natural way."

" Ilka man buckles his belt to his ain gaet. They wha ha' to deal wi' savages maun be savages their ain selves," said Stewart.

" This is horrible! to hear civilized people with the Bible in their houses, and professing Christianity, talking like savages, and resolving to train up the children of Christian parents like a butcher's dog," replied Honeywood. " I've said more than once, that I believed, if we'd been brought up as the Indians are, we should have been just like them; but I never expected to hear Christian men avowing Indian sentiments, and, because they have to deal with them, resolving to bring up their children as the savage does his. I expect the next move will be to learn them to eat human flesh, as the savage does on some special occasions. I can't but think more is expected of us, both by God and man, than of them. I don't believe we are to measure our conduct towards them by their conduct to us, and teach our children to do the same. Indeed, I shall now begin to think, that, according to their light and knowledge, they are, on the whole, better than the whites. They won't steal from or lie to one another, but the whites will. They will divide the last crust with a friend or a stranger: not every white man will. They never forget a kindness: white men often do. A worm will turn when it is trodden upon; and we need not to be told what provocations have been given them. I, for one, have received much kindness from Indians; and I know some of them whom I would as soon trust with property, or even my life, as my own neighbors."

"Oh, Ned Honeywood! you've only seen the best side on 'em, when they were good-natured, or had some selfish ends ter serve. But let 'em break inter your house, murder your wife, take that youngest child of yours up by the heels, and smash its brains out on the door-stone, and then see if you wouldn't, as Blanchard says, take it the nat'ral way, and hate 'em as bad as me or McClure, or Grant or Stewart. I wouldn't give much for the life of an Indian within range of your rifle arter that. I'm afeard, my son, you'll rue the day you allowed your good nature ter git the upper hand, and put so much trust in 'em."

"If the Indians should do as you say (and I have no doubt they would if it was war between us), I should kill them if I could; but I should not hate and shoot every Indian I came across after that, and who had no hand in the matter."

"I reckon, now, you put as much confidence in that Mohawk you hunted with so long on the Juniata, as in any of us."

"Just as much."

"Well, it's my candid opinion that fellow would lead a squad of savages down here to take your scalp and mine, as quick as any of 'em."

"The Six Nations," said Honeywood, "have not joined the French, nor dug up the hatchet. It is the Delawares, Shawanees, Monseys, and other broken tribes, that fought Braddock, and have come down on the frontiers. If his people were at war with us, I should expect the Mohawk to fight on his own side, and I should on ours; but, that he would do any thing more than that, I don't believe."

"He'd take your scalp the instant the war-post was struck, and his Indian blood was up, or roast you by a slow fire out of friendship, and ter give you a chance ter show your courage."

"Delawares or not," said Grant, " the Indians that attacked us in the gap of the Blue Mountains were led by a Seneca, the fellow with a red breech-cloth; and the Senecas belong to the Six Nations."

"That's so," said McClure; "but the rest on 'em were Delawares."

"I have no doubt," said Honeywood, " that it is difficult for the chiefs to restrain their young men, and that once in a while the Mohawks, Senecas, and Oneidas join the parties of Delawares; and if something is not done, and that speedily, by our people, the influence of the French and the passions of the young warriors will overpower the authority of the old chiefs, and we shall have all the Indian tribes upon us."

"And then the folks who thinks an Indian's sich a lovely critter 'll git all they want of 'em," said Holdness.

It happened singularly enough, that though McClure was hot tempered, about as rough a specimen of frontier breeding as you would care to meet, and often in difficulties on his own account, in regard to any little difference of feeling among his neighbors he generally acted the part of peacemaker.

Notwithstanding his strong points, impulsive temperament, and rough exterior, McClure was true metal, and universally respected and beloved by his neighbors; and between him and Holdness, who had been comrades in many a hard fight, there existed a firm attachment. He was open as the day, kind-hearted, and generous; and though cherishing those bitter prejudices against the Indians, common to all the frontier inhabitants, there lurked beneath that rough exterior, deep religious convictions, being thoroughly imbued with the doctrines of the Kirk of Scotland, though it must be confessed they exerted at times but very little influence on his practice. But McClure had this about him: he did love a person whom he believed to be a Christian man, wanted others to be better than himself, struggled hard with his savage temper, and had the courage and nobleness, when he knew he had done a wrong thing, to acknowledge it.

Strong as were the passions and prejudices of the old rough, his judgment was excellent; and he saw clearly the absolute necessity of the most entire unanimity of sentiment among their small number, surrounded as they were by peril. He also cherished a great love for Honeywood, although they were in most respects as unlike as two men could well be.

Thus McClure possessed an influence with the rougher sort by reason of his likeness to them, and with the serious-minded because they knew he was right at the core.

There were many points of dissimilarity between Honeywood and the rude spirits among whom it may be truly said he was sown by the winds. Not having been born in the country, he had not drawn in with his mother's milk, and learned at his father's knee, those bitter sentiments in respect to the Indians prevalent among them. On the other hand, he had received from the Quakers, and from intercourse with the Indians themselves, ideas directly the reverse.

Honeywood had also received a common-school education, was a thoroughly religious man, anxious that the children and youth who were growing up in ignorance, altogether occupied in hunting and fighting, should obtain some schooling, and that kind of religious instruction calculated to neutralize the savage lessons they were taught, both by the precepts and examples of their elders.

These were great differences, and of that nature which generally produces alienation; but there were influences, equally potent, of an opposite tendency.

Honeywood possessed great strength, activity, and courage. With passions violent as those of Holdness or McClure, he united the most entire self-control; and no emergency, however great, could confuse or throw him into trepidation. Among a community of sharp-shooters, he stood without a rival. He could draw the bow or fling the tomahawk with the dexterity of an Indian, and converse in several of the Indian dialects. In his boyhood he had been apprenticed to a gunsmith, could repair a rifle, shoe a horse, mend plough irons, and make an edge-tool.

If any of our young friends wish to know more of his early history, they must consult the first volume of this series.

CHAPTER IV.

MCCLURE A PEACEMAKER.

JUST as Honeywood was about to reply, McClure, beckoning him to remain quiet, interposed in his own blunt way, "Brad Holdness, Honeywood's right, and you're wrong; and when I say that I take in my ain sell."

McClure was apt to get to his Scotch when in earnest.

"And the women have the right of it too," continued he, "as they always do amaist. Grant, Armstrong, and old Mac [Maccoy] are about of a muchness. Israel Blanchard's worse, 'cause he's had more privileges and not sae muckle provocation, seeing a good deal of what he knows has been handed down to him from his forbears; but wi' us it's bitter experience, and we are wrong, though I don't deny it's human natur. But, to come right down to the real fine thing, Honeywood is right, when he says there's more to be expected of us than of the Indians, 'cause we wasn't nursed by the wolves, but had Christian mothers, and we know what they taught us; and yet when he says we are as bad as they are, and are evening oursel's to them, he says what's true; for God help the Indian, squaw or pappoose or baldhead, that falls into our hands, if we git the better of 'em!

"He says we're tryin' to train up the bairns in the same gaet, which is true likewise. Now, we know it's clean agin' conscience, though we've done it sae many times, and gi'en our conscience sae many sair strokes, it ha' just the breath o' life in it: still it's alive, and I'm free to say Mr. Honeywood has stirred mine mair than it's been stirred for mony a day."

"He may be richt; but what is richt may not be expedient," said Stewart.

"Ay; but it is in this matter, since it has been proved that in respect to the degree Maister Honeywood has managed to git his notions into the bairns and the lads, it has made them no worse for fighting, scouting-labor, or dutifulness, but better in all these respects; and, if ony man can say I'm far frae the richt, let him say it."

"And, if Israel don't say the same, I'll say it for him," said Mrs. Blanchard; "for I've heard him say a hundred times before we came into garrison that he was always glad to have our boys go over to Mr. Honeywood's, because they always brought something good home with 'em."

"You may weel think (for you all ken what kind of a wild beast Sandie McClure is when his bluid's up) that what I'm goin' to say niest gaes sairly across the grain.

"We once had a good man, a douce, sensible Christian man, dwellin' along wi' us, who had prayers night and morning: sae do we Scotch people read the Scripture, and sing a psalm, as our mithers ha' taught us; but we do it just for auld custom; but we dinna pray, sin' 'twould be the prayer o' the wicked, and would not be heard. He held meetings among us often whiles. He was a head o' wheat growin' up among the tares. But for our wickedness, and because we would not hearken to him, the Lord took him frae us; and those were bitter tears that fell into his grave.

"Then there was Ephraim Cuthbert: all allow he was a righteous man, though he had silly notions. He had to leave the land he loved richt weel, because he was afraid his children would grow up as ignorant and bluidthirsty as ours. I s'pose I did as much to insult and drive him off, and more, than any other man, and I've been richt sorry for it. But that's neither here nor there: he was nothin' for defence, and sae no loss in that respect.

"But here's Maister Honeywood, who's nae Quaker, but a man to be counted on in the day o' tribulation, when a man's mair precious than gold, — no mair flinch about him than an oak-tree on the flank o' the Alleghanies.

"When we were between the wolves and the deep sea; when it seemed death to bide, and but little better to flit, — some were for biding, mair were for ganging, and some were spiering what ither folk wad do, — up gets Maister Honeywood like an auld Hieland chief, and shouts, 'If every man, woman, and bairn forsakes this Run, I'll stay, and die for the ground!' That settled the matter."

"That's so!" said Armstrong. "For then I made up my mind to fight it out, and I'm of the same mind still."

"There's mair than that," said McClure. "He's a good smith, can shoe a mule, and, what is more consequence to us, he can mend a gun, make a knife and tomahawk, and new lay an axe.

"He's a Christian man, prays night and morning, learns the lads good things; he's for every thing worthy, and, if he was encouraged, would do mair still. We could afford to lose Ephraim Cuthbert, as far as fighting went; though, whether we could afford to lose his prayers and good example, I will not tak' upon me to say.

"Maister Honeywood has a mind of his ain, a young family comin' on; he'll not have 'em brought up in the way that has been talked about here to-night. He'll flit when he canna bear it longer, and the bairns get somewhat older; and, whether we can afford to part wi' him, you can judge as weel as mysel."

"Don't talk about Mr. Honeywood's going away; for I know my Harry and all the other boys would follow him, and never ask for what or where," said Mrs. Sumerford.

"I ha' but one word mair, and then I ha' done. Nat is back here among us because he loved the boys he was brought up wi', and the house he was born in; but, though he's no Quaker now as to many things, yet he is not like mysel' and the maist of us, but mair like Maister Honeywood, who was all the friend his father had one while; and it's not civil to him or Maister Honeywood to be casting up to them any notions o' their ain, when they are ready to shed their bluid in our defence ; or to be makin' free with the fashion in which they were brought up. I ken it is not richt, to begin wi'; and I leave Jamie Stewart to let us ken gin it wad be *expedient.*"

Compelled by his shrewd countryman to speak, and also to assent to the views of the former, Stewart made answer in that guarded manner in which a Scotchman is wont to express himself.

"I canna tak' upon me to speak precisely in respect to what ye spier, Sandie McClure; but I am free to say sae much as this; nae doubt what is bred in the bone is ill to come out o' the flesh ; and he that comes o' the hens maun scratch. The bairns they see all that's done, hear all that's said, and know all their parents feel, and do likewise. Such auld sinners as mysel' and some ithers canna be blown about like windle straes by a breath o' the mouth ; but there's no need o' our haudin' off, and settin' a back fire, and fellin' trees across the road Maister Honeywood and the good wives want the children to travel in.

"We can say what we ken to be true, that a little mair knowledge, civility, and God's grace, if he should see fit to gie it, wad mak' them nae worse, but better, baith for this world and the next, because no man will deny but life is held by a very small thread among us just at present. There'll be some gude done, though it may be long comin'; for, spit on a stone, it'll be wet at last. I dinna opine the little spats that whiles come up atween us are mair than skin deep, just clishmaclavers, clouds across the sun."

"That's it," said Holdness. "Ned won't mind me, or what I say: he's more *sense*."

Mrs. Blanchard was a sincerely pious woman, and had in her New England home received a common-school education. Her husband, Israel Blanchard, was a firm believer in the truths of the gospel, a very intelligent man, but had in early life lived on the frontiers of New England, lost many of his relatives by the savages, and, — though a man of kindly feelings and an excellent neighbor, — like the great majority of the New England settlers who were constantly brought in contact with Indians, viewed them as past redemption, and fit only to be exterminated. Thus, although esteeming the sentiments of Honeywood in respect to the treatment of Indians, and any virtues they might possess, as mere moonshine in water, he respected and loved the man, and was conscious that his own example and conversation both injured the feelings of his wife, to whom he was tenderly attached, and exerted a wretched influence upon his children. He therefore held his peace as the wisest course, and permitted his wife to represent him.

Mrs. Blanchard taught the school, the settlers having built a schoolhouse inside the stockade. She was in perfect sympathy with Honeywood in his plans of improvement, and very anxious that those kindly feelings now in the ascendancy should not evaporate with the occasion, especially as she perceived that the religious convictions of McClure, Stewart, and others, were now aroused.

"Neighbors," she observed, "when we were building the schoolhouse, and after it was finished, many of us said and hoped, that, now we had so good a place, we might have meetings on the sabbath. We certainly ought to do so. Some of us have professed to be God's people, and long for it. It is true that we observe the sabbath in respect that we neither work the land, nor hunt; but, aside from that, we on the whole live like heathen. I know we've had a great deal to break us up, — Indian rumors and attacks, scouting and watching night and day, and but little rest for any one. Now the Lord has given us a snow-storm, and some relief from the Indians while it lasts; and I feel we ought to improve the opportunity as he would have us. There's plenty can sing. Israel will lift the tune: he used to do it in Vermont. There are many of the boys would make good singers, — Harry Sumerford for one."

"I don't know how ter read: how could I sing?" said Harry.

"How do you sing so many songs?" said his mother.

"Oh! I can learn them by heart, hearin' other folks sing 'em."

"Well, you can learn hymns the same way."

"You know you are going to learn to read," said Honeywood.

"I go in for that," said Holdness. "Ned kin read a sarmon, and pray; my wife kin pray too; and Mrs. Blanchard's got a sarmon-book, and Ned kin read out of that."

"I was near saying the same thing mysel', that we might have a meetin', but thought I was not the one ter say it. I ha' a sermon-book my father brought from Scotland. I've strapped my razor on it more than once, but now I'll put it to a better use," said McClure.

"There are many things we might ha' put to a better use than we ha' done, Sandie McClure," replied Stewart,—"our own conscience for one thing, and the lessons our forbears taught us for anither. My auld mither wad ha' wanted her daily bread rather than missed being in her seat at the kirk on sabbath morning. We bring ower their buiks, and we leave their principles ahint [behind] us; but I'm weel pleased wi' the turn things are takin' just at this present."

The little ripple that had disturbed the usual harmony of their intercourse having subsided, they made an agreement for a meeting on the next sabbath, and retired to rest far better satisfied with themselves and each other than before.

CHAPTER V.

SHALL WE HAVE THE GIRLS?

FOR the first time since going into garrison, there was no watch kept, but every eye was closed in peaceful slumber. Through the long night no sound broke the universal stillness, save the rending of limbs in the forest, borne down by the burden of snow, and the occasional bark of a dog. When they awoke the next morning, it was to a jubilee. The sun from a cloudless sky was flinging his beams over a landscape of dazzling whiteness.

The mountains, the branches of the great hemlocks massed together in clusters, and the roofs of the buildings, were all covered with the fleecy mantle.

With a tremendous uproar, the boys leaped from bed as the sunlight shone into the loop-holes, flung on their clothes, thrust their feet into moccasons; and, finding the great gate of the stockade wide open, the crazy creatures who had been so long confined within garrison-walls, or allowed partial liberty, rushed out pell-mell, screaming, laughing, diving into the snow, rolling over in it, pelting one another with snow-balls, and wild with joy; while even the parents themselves, those stern warriors with wounds half healed, and who had of late pulled so many fatal triggers, engaged in a downright game of snowballing.

Beholding the frolicking of those veterans who had been in Indian fights times without number, several of them in the army, and whom they had been wont to regard with awe, and hoped some day to be like, the children could contain themselves no longer.

"Oh, see my father!"

"Oh, see Mr. Proctor!" resounded on all sides.

"Zuckers!" shouted Tony: "Mr. Holdness hit my father right in the mouth."

"Oh, my!" screamed Johnnie Crawford. "Mr. McClure fired at Mr. Honeywood; and he jumped up in the air, and it went right 'twixt his legs,—it did."

In their abandonment they hugged their parents' legs, and then rolled over in the snow.

Just then, as though there was not sufficient going on, an enormous wolf-dog, followed by nine pups and three bear-cubs, appeared on the field.

"Here comes Mr. Honeywood's Kate and her puppies!" cried Johnnie Crawford.

"And my bear and Tony's babies!" cried Sam Sumerford.

The dogs enjoyed the fun hugely, barking, leaping, and wagging their tails as though they would wag them off; and, indeed, so did the bears, except Tony's, who was of a different disposition from the two others, and would not submit to impositions. Ike Proctor got this bear down on his back, and was proceeding to rub snow in his face, when the cub gave Ike a blow with his paw that make him see sparks, and bellow loudly.

"I wouldn't cry, Ike," said Johnnie Crawford. "I didn't cry when the bullet hitted me in the leg."

"No more would I if a bullet hit me: I wouldn't touch to; but guess you'd cry if a bear hit you. I tell you it hurts." Ike put his hand to his cheek, that was bleeding a little from the impression of the bear's claws.

While the fun was at its height, the shrill voices

of several women, pitched in the highest key, rose above the din. Turning suddenly round, Holdness beheld all the female portion of the garrison looking on with the greatest interest.

"Come, Israel!" cried Mrs. Blanchard. "We've been screaming ourselves hoarse for you men-folks to come to breakfast: the victuals 'll be as cold as a stone."

"Don't care if they are: we're warm enough to make it up. I'm bound to get even with McClure, then I'll come."

"And I," said Stewart, "maun gie Proctor the snowballs I've made up." He had three in the breast of his hunting-shirt, and three more under his left arm.

"I thought you calculated to kill the hogs to-day," said Mrs. Holdness. "If you do, it's time breakfast was out of the way, and the water heating. You've got to kill one hog, at any rate; that is, if you expect to have any thing to eat to-morrow."

"Away with you," shouted Honeywood, "spoiling all the fun!"

He let fly a snowball, that, hitting the gate just over his wife's head, broke in pieces, sprinkling the snow on her bare head and arms. McClure and Blanchard followed suit; and the women, laughing and screaming, took to their heels.

"The hogs, the hogs!" shouted Ike, scrambling to his feet, and dismissing all thought of the injury he had received: "they be goin' ter kill the hogs, and there won't be no schule, 'cause the schule-ma'am said there wouldn't when they killed the hogs."

"We'll have the bladders," said Dan Mugford, "and blow 'em up, and put peas in 'em, and kick 'em for footballs."

"We'll fix some for our mothers to put lard in, and bear's grease: they be real nice for that," said Nat Holt.

"They be right good when anybody's wounded: they put warm water in 'em, and then they put a goose-quill in the neck on 'em, and squirt the water inter the wound, and clean it all out," said Sandie Maccoy.

"We'll git the brussels [bristles] what grows on the hogs' backs," said Archie Crawford: "father knows how to make brushes on 'em ter brush out the pans of the rifles; and they're good to sow [sew] saddles with."

"I know somethin' don't none of you know," said Ben Wood: "Mr. Holdness's goin' to kill an ox, 'cause he's got a wolf comin' on his jaw; and Cal said how I might have his bladder; and an ox's bladder's as big as three hogs'."

A "wolf" is a species of wen that sometimes grows on the jaw of an ox, and does not injure the carcass for meat if the animal is butchered in season.

"When I lived at home," said Willie Redmond, "and father killed the hogs, I used ter git the tails, and bake 'em in the ashes. Tails is raal good, I tell you."

"If our ma'ams won't let us bake 'em in the fire," said Tony, "we'll go down ter Mr. Cuthbert's house, and make a big fire, and roast 'em there; and we kin screech and tear round when we're eatin' 'em; and we kin go in the evenin' too, and have pitchwood lights, 'cause there ain't no Injuns round now."

"We kin carry some taters, and bake 'em, and some corn to parch, and maple sugar," said Ike.

"Shall we have Scip?" inquired Sammy.

"With course: we couldn't have no good time 'thout Scip; and we'll have some eggs, and roast 'em in the ashes, 'cause Scip loves eggs; and he'll cut the wood for us ter make the fire, and roll in the big logs," said Will Rogers.

Scip was a slave belonging to Israel Blanchard.

"Shall we have the gals?" said Archie Crawford.

"I wouldn't," said Sammy: "gals ain't no good. We can't do a good many things if we have 'em."

"I would have 'em," said Tony. "I want ter have our Maud and Jean: they'll help us a lot; they know 'bout cooking better nor we do. We couldn't have killed the McDonalds 'thout them."

"Yes, we could too; and if we hadn't had 'em their mothers wouldn't have found us out, and I and Sammy wouldn't have got such an awful lickin'. 'Twill be jest so agin if we have 'em: their mothers'll miss 'em, and come after 'em right in the middle jest when we be havin' the goodest time, and break it all up. I don't see the good of havin' gals stickin' in everywhere: let 'em stay ter home 'long their mothers and the babies," said Ike Proctor.

"So I think," said Fred Stiefel.

"That's 'cause you ain't got any sisters," said Nat Holt. "Gals want ter have some good times 's well as we do. We have all the good times there be: soon 's the gals git out of school they have ter go right in the house and work, and take kere of the babies. Havin' supper down there won't be a mite like killin' the McDonalds. Their mothers won't think it any hurt for 'em to go there and play, and they won't think of comin' arter 'em nor us neither; but killin' the McDonalds, they all said, was the worst thing ever could be."

"I want our Alice to come," said Jim Grant. "Hold up your hands, and be counted, all what want the gals to come."

Five, out of thirteen, held up their hands. "They can't come, and I'm glad," said Sam Sumerford.

Tony seemed for a moment very much disconcerted. His resources, however, were usually equal to the occasion; and they were not wanting in this exigency. After a few moments spent in reflection, he said, "Zuckers! you'll wish you had let 'em come, 'cause they'll ax us, and we shall say we wanted ter have 'em, but you fellers wouldn't; then they'll be mad with you, and when they have honey and maple sugar, and their mothers let 'em cook, and make custards and fry doughnuts, you won't git one mite; but we shall."

"I don't kere," said Sammy. "I don't want any of their things: my marm'll make me good things."

"I care," said Dan Mugford. "Tony, if we'll all hold up our hands, won't you tell 'em any thing about what we've said?"

"No, I won't truly."

Upon which all held up their hands but Sammy; who, finding himself alone in the opposition, at length reluctantly held up his hand.

CHAPTER VI.

NO SCHOOL, AND PLENTY OF FUN.

AT that moment a snowball struck Tony on the side of the head; and the lads, looking in the direction from whence it came, saw Scip standing in the gate, who shouted,—

"What for you no come breakfast, you boys? Men-folks gone done eber so long. Massa Blanchard makin' tongs; Massa Holdness and Cal grind de knives. Harry and de boys, dey gone to de woods to git de pole hang de hogs on. You boys dere sky-larkin' in de snow when dey want you to bring de rocks put in de fire. 'Shamed of you, I is. Tink you'd know better'n dat, when dere's so much to be done."

When the boys finally reached the house, they found every one fully occupied. McClure had been chosen head man, and had assigned to each division their several duties.

Israel Blanchard had just finished making three pairs of wooden tongs, some ten feet in length, of saplings flattened at the jaws, and fastened with a wooden pin at the joints.

In a few moments Harry, Alex., Enoch Sumerford, Hugh Crawford, jun., and Armstrong brought into the stockade, on their shoulders, an ash-tree full forty feet in length, and eight inches in diameter at the butt, and flung it down.

Next came Grant, Holt, Wood, and Stewart, with a load of stones, on an ox-sled, that they had procured from some large heaps in Cuthbert's field, by digging away the snow.

When the garrison was built, the settlers had made several huge troughs that were kept full of water from the spring, in case of siege, when the Indians were accustomed to attack with fire-arrows.

They were also accustomed to use large troughs for most of the purposes for which barrels, hogsheads, and boxes of all kinds are now used. In these were pickled pork, beef, and hams; soap, maple sugar, grain, and corn were also kept in them.

Before the Blanchards came, bringing a whip-saw, they had no way to manufacture a board but by splitting it from a log, and then it was a clumsy affair; and now, though they had a whip-saw, it was a good deal of work to saw out boards; and troughs were used about as much as before.

Harry Sumerford, Holdness, and some others, made small tubs for washing, and pails and large kegs to hold about fifteen gallons, to be carried on mules; large wooden hooks being fastened to the pack-saddles in which the kegs were placed, one on each side. They also manufactured a concern called a wooden bottle, which was a flat keg with staves about eight inches in length, but with heads the size of a half-barrel; being flat, they were well fitted to go into the pockets of the pack-saddles. But there was not a box, barrel, hogshead, or large tub to be found in Wolf Run at this time; since soon after the Blanchards came with the whip-saw, and by the time they had manufactured a few boards for tables, doors, and other necessary uses, the Indian war broke out. The whip-saw was exchanged for the rifle; and many a fond plan of improvement, cherished by the Blanchards and others, ended in smoke.

The mere preservation of life was about all that now occupied men's thoughts: even that was held by a most uncertain tenure.

So destitute were they now of articles considered then of absolute necessity, that among them all there was not a pot that would hold over two pailfuls.

Some boys who will read this story live on farms, and know something about the methods in which work is there done; and I should like to ask them how they expect these Wolf Run folks are going to kill and dress twenty-five hogs, with scarcely any of those appliances considered at the present day absolutely necessary.

We shall see; for one thing is certain: whatever such people undertake to do will be done. Remember Harry Sumerford's drum in "Brought to the Front."

The women and children, aided by Scipio, had already made a great fire in the garrison, put on the crane and what kettles they could muster filled with water.

In one corner of the stockade the snow had been scraped away, and another large fire built. The troughs were all brought out, and platforms made beside them (on which to lay the hogs) by piling up some blocks, and laying upon them the doors of the flankers, schoolhouse, blacksmith-shop, the great gate of the garrison, and the window-shutters, all of which were made either of plank manufactured with the whip-saw, or timber hewed to a proud edge with the broad-axe, thus presenting a smooth surface.

The utilizing of the outside gate in this way left the cattle at liberty, who, rejoicing in their freedom after so long confinement, spread themselves over the fields, tails in the air, bellowing, snorting, and chasing the puppies, who instantly set upon them, but were soon glad to turn tail to, in order to escape the hoofs and horns of the liberated beasts; while the bears, unnoticed by the children, sought the nearest wood, and were soon sunning themselves in the top of a large white oak.

A great many stones were made red hot in these two fires, and then plunged into the troughs that had been filled with cold water; and in a very few moments the water was brought to a boil, and the work of slaughtering began in earnest; for there was no lack of strong hands well accustomed to the work.

A few hot rocks were put in from time to time, in order to maintain the heat; and thus the same water served for scalding a good many hogs. The women and children brought from the house the water that was heated in the kettles, put the rocks into the fires, and likewise supplied the fires with wood.

The large wooden tongs made by Blanchard were now set up, the legs spread wide apart, and the ends secured in the ground, after which the great pole was lifted up, and placed in the open jaws; and as soon as a hog was stripped of bristles he was hung on the poles, and dressed.

In another part of the yard Heinrich Stiefel, Honeywood, and Proctor were performing a very different operation; for, instead of scalding, they covered the body of their hog with straw cut short, and then set fire to it, burning off all the bristles, after which they poured on clean hot water from the kettles, and scraped the whole surface with sharp knives.

The only objection to this method was, that the roots of the bristles were left in the skin; whereas when the animal was scalded they came out. It, however, expedited business very much, as there were not troughs enough for all to work at.

To the great delight of the children, it soon became evident that the work could not be completed in a single day, as much time had been consumed in getting ready to work; and also that it would not be possible for Mrs. Blanchard to keep school, as the butchering made her presence necessary at home.

"We can't finish to-day: 'twill take part of another day," said McClure. "So we might as well knock off in good season; for the women are tired, and want to clear up a little."

The first hog dressed in the morning had been split through the brisket, and plentifully soused with cold water, after which two parallel incisions were made each side of the backbone, from the tail to the head, and reaching to the ribs in depth, in order to admit the air, and remove the animal heat.

The carcass hung thus till after dinner, when the ribs were cut through, and the backbone with the lean meat and pork attached taken out the whole length of the hog, and placed on the snow to cool.

Here were some nice pieces which the good wives lost no time in cooking; and that night the whole company sat down to a bountiful supper of fresh meat.

So merry were they, what with the fresh meat, the salt, and the snowstorm, that even Simon Lombard caught the infection, forgot his sorrows, and told stories of his adventures as an Indian trader, that greatly interested and amused his entertainers; and finally Stewart led off with " Auld Lang Syne ; " all who could sing, heartily joining.

It was a joyous reaction, consequent upon the sudden relief from constant apprehension and unceasing watchfulness, both day and night.

I suppose my young readers may think that when supper was finished, and the household had arranged themselves around the room for a social evening's chat, the children sat listening to the stories that were told by one and another.

That indeed was the case for an hour or so ; but by and by the children, accidentally of course, were together in a corner behind the long table, engaged in a whispered conversation, which, actuated by the laudable desire of throwing light upon events both past, present, and future, we shall venture to communicate.

"Have you ax'd your ma'ams ? " said Tony,

who generally took the lead in all affairs of moment.

"I ax'd mine," said Sam : "she'll let *me* go."

"So will mine let me go," said Fred Stiefel.

Nearly all of them had asked their mothers, and received permission, and their sisters were also allowed to accompany them; but only on condition that there should be no Indian didos, no scalping, tomahawking, painting of faces, and no scaring of Scipio.

"My mother says that we can't do any thing we like in that house as we have done, 'cause Nat Cuthbert's here now, and will have something ter say 'bout it; and we must git his consent," observed Archie Crawford.

"He'll let us play there, I know," said Will Redmond, " 'cause he's just as clever's he kin be ; and I'll git Cal Holdness to ax him: he'll do any thing for Cal 'cause he bathes his arm, and cuts his vittles."

"Git Prudence to ax him: he'll do more for her than he will for Cal or anybody," said Dan Mugford.

"When shall we have it?" said Jim Grant.

"To-morrow night," said Sam.

"No, we can't nuther," said Tony, "'cause we want ter see 'em kill the hogs to-morrow, and git the bladders; and the day arter that we've got ter go ter schule; and we can't git ready for it in one day, and go ter schule too. We must wait till they kill the hogs, and cut 'em up; and then have it."

The conclave now dissolved, and the children mingled with their elders. In a few moments Sam Sumerford approached the fire with a ball of wet clay in his fist, which, after raking open the embers, he proceeded to deposit and cover up in hot ashes and coals. In the course of half an hour the mysterious Sam appeared again, and taking the clay that was now burned hard, with the tongs, flung it out of doors into the snow, followed this time by all the rest.

When cool enough to handle, and while the attention of the older portion of the company was occupied with the singing, the junk of burnt clay was conveyed to the retreat behind the table.

One blow with a stone, the clay split in halves; out rolled a pig's appendage, and the grateful odor of roast pork was diffused through the room.

Sammy now proceeded, with the scalping-knife,

to divide it into thirteen pieces (and it was not a very long tail either), and distributed them among his companions, reserving the smallest piece for himself.

It was but a morsel to each; yet that morsel was sweet because a foretaste of what the future held in store, and a great deal better than any thing their mothers could cook.

"Ain't these good times?" cried Will Redmond, hugging Sammy in the fulness of his heart. "I never had any sich good times afore in my life."

Many times during the day had the children promenaded beside the long row of defunct swine hourly increasing, with raised hopes, and eyes eagerly fastened upon that portion of the animal most interesting to them, but still not daring to meddle.

When, however, Sammy saw McClure cutting into pieces the long strip reserved from the first hog killed, to cook for supper, and observed his mother take up the portion that contained the appendage, he followed her into the house, and teased till he got it.

The work was finished the next day by the middle of the afternoon.

That long row of well-dressed porkers strung on the pole, each with a corn-cob stuck as though in mockery between his jaws, was a spectacle well pleasing to the settlers, and suggestive of plenty, especially as there were many more hogs left in the pens, — old breeders, shoats too young to butcher, and late pigs.

The main dependence of the settlers, both for their own support and also for obtaining needed supplies from the older settlements, was upon the hog crop.

Neither wheat nor corn would pay to transport long distances through forests and over mountains on pack-horses; but hams and flitches of bacon would, and bring cash, or they could be bartered for salt, iron, wool-cards, or whatever they might need. So would maple sugar and potash; but they had not kettles to manufacture either of these articles except in small quantities, and by dint of great labor and contrivance.

Cattle could be transported, because they might be driven, and sold on the hoof; but to produce fat cattle requires luxuriant pastures and cultivated grasses, and the settlement was too recent for that.

Honeywood had by great effort obtained a little English grass-seed from a German at Philadelphia, and was now every year raising a little seed; and, as soon as the decay of the roots and stumps permitted, he ploughed his ground. But the majority pursued a very different method. They planted corn, and sowed grass on burns, or else, after the corn was off, scratched the ground between the stumps with a plough, and sowed grain. Then the land was left for the grass "to come in of itself," as it was termed; that, is to grow up to weeds of all sorts, and wild grass, and bushes; part of it reserved for mowing, and the rest for pasture.

It is easy to see that not much hay would be cut to winter the cattle. Some wild grass was cut in the swamps, by the streams, and on old beaver-dams; some corn was fed out; and yellow-birch and maple trees were cut down, and the cattle ate the buds and small twigs. The result was that in the spring the stock came out poor; many cattle died, especially the yearlings.

But, in respect to hogs, it was altogether another affair. Corn in large quantities, and grain too, could be raised on the burns: nothing to do but fell the trees, put in the fire, make a hole with a stake, and drop in the kernels, and cover them with your toe.

When the settler had succeeded in raising the first crop of corn, he could begin to keep hogs. All through the spring and summer, the pigs would get the greater part of their own living in the woods and pastures. If there was any grass growing in the openings they would find it; tear the rotten logs to pieces after worms, grubs, and wood-mice; find rattlesnakes and thistle-roots; and they needed only a little corn and milk, now and then, through all the spring and summer.

When autumn came they would fatten on beech-nuts, acorns, and other nuts and berries; requiring but a little corn to harden the pork, and take away the oily taste.

You see the temptation to slovenly farming. Thus the common custom in all the frontier settlements was to keep all the hogs possible, raise corn on the burns to carry them through the winter, kill every bear, deer, wild pigeon, and coon that could be found, to help the pork-trough, so as to have the more pork to market; and the moment fur was prime in the fall,—instead of ploughing, getting out stumps and rocks, working over the old burns, and killing weeds and bushes, — to saddle the horses, load them with traps, and start off on a winter's hunt; for a pack of furs that a hunter could carry on his back would bring more money than four mule-loads of bacon.

It was the passion for hunting and trapping, every year growing more precarious, that gave the death-blow to all progress in the cultivation of the soil, the only real strength of a community.

This fondness for the woods, with both young and old, Honeywood was endeavoring to overcome, and to encourage love for the soil and desire for knowledge. He had succeeded in a measure with the Sumerford boys and some others, and had all the women in sympathy with him, also McClure, Stewart, Heinrich, Stiefel, the Blanchards, and Holdness, who had been led to see, that, after all, farming was the main shaft; and they were struggling hard to crucify their wild instincts,— that is, McClure and Holdness. The Indian outbreak, however, seemed likely to unsettle every thing, and throw the whole community back upon the rifle and tomahawk.

CHAPTER VII.

HENS ACCUSED OF PREVARICATION.

THE moment Honeywood entered the kitchen the next morning, he was grappled by Tony and Will Redmond, who besought him to cut off the tails of all the hogs, and commit the treasure to them; and by persistent effort they gained their point.

The hogs were now to be cut up, the shoulders and hams cut out and trimmed, and the meat salted. As much of the lean meat as it was supposed could be eaten fresh, was to be packed in snow, in order to economize the salt.

A portion of the settlers began to cut up the pork. Israel Blanchard, Honeywood, and Proctor went into the woods with the cattle, to cut and haul small-sized logs to build a smoke-house to cure the bacon in.

Harry, Will Grant, Cal Holdness, and Scipio

were sent into the forest in another direction, to fall trees for the cattle to browse on in order to save the hay; and they took the cattle along with them.

The instinct displayed by the cattle was worthy of notice. When they saw the boys with axes on their shoulders, starting for the woods, the greater part of them followed, capering, and manifesting their gratification. A few, however, lingered around the gate, roaring and snorting as they smelt of the ground still bearing traces of recent slaughter; but, the moment they heard the crash of the first tree as it fell, they likewise went galloping to share in the anticipated feast.

The children, having matters of far greater import pressing upon their minds, evinced but little interest in these preparations, and sauntered reluctantly to school, counting their steps and quite silent.

Harry and his mates had not been chopping more than half an hour when they missed the negro.

"What's become of Scip, Cal?" said Will Grant.

"Don't know. Guess he's gone to the spring to git a drink: should like one myself."

"Look here! see the sap run out of this tree we've jest cut: wonder if a feller couldn't git a drink of maple-sap."

"Guess it's too early for that."

"There's a sugar-tree," said Will, "stands right in the sun. Stick your axe in him, Harry, and I'll make a trough."

Harry with an upward stroke drove his axe into the tree, and watched the result. In a few moments, the sap began to ooze slowly from the wound, and trickle along the blade of the axe, till at length it dropped from the pole.

"It's coming, Will: fetch on your trough."

Cal now cut a large chip, sharpened one end in the form of a wedge, hollowed the middle with his knife to guide the sap, and drove it into the incision. The trough was placed under this rude spout, from which, nevertheless, the sap began to drop faster and faster. They made another trough, put in a second spout, and resumed their work.

"Scip's been long enough gittin' his drink. I guess he's afraid of Indians: the most he thinks about is Indians," said Will.

Two hours had passed when Cal exclaimed, "We've cut enough: look at the cattle."

Having filled themselves, they were now finding amusement in hooking the tree-tops, breaking off large limbs with their horns, and running about with them on their heads; the oxen getting down on their knees, roaring, and running their horns in among the brush; but the bull, standing aloof in his pride of place, was bellowing, arching his great neck, flinging the snow over his flanks with his fore-feet, and challenging the whole Province of Pennsylvania to the combat; while a meek-eyed heifer stood quietly chewing her cud, and gazing upon the champions in humble admiration.

"There ain't much Quaker blood in that bull, if Ephraim Cuthbert did raise him," said Harry.

"I don't know about the blood," said Will; "for Nat's as full of fight as that bull, and he was Quaker born and bred."

"That's what they've both got by keepin' bad company, and mixin' up with us Wolf Run folks: after all Mr. Honeywood's pains, we ain't much better'n wild beasts," said Cal. "Come, let's go home."

"I won't," said Will. "Let's set down in the sun, and cool off. I want a drink of sap afore I go."

Putting on their clothes, they sat down on a knoll from which the snow had thawed, and waited till there was sap enough in the trough to afford them a drink all round.

"Hark!" said Harry as they rose up to go, "I hear an axe going down to Cuthbert's: let's take a slant over that way."

As the party came in sight of the house, they discovered Scipio, stripped to shirt and trousers, making the chips fly at a merry rate.

"We won't go near," said Cal. "The children are goin' down to the house to have some kind of doings, and I'll warrant they've laid in with Scip to cut the wood for 'em. The creature'll do most any thing the children want him to."

"He's cunning enough to take this chance," said Harry. "If Mr. Blanchard had been with us he wouldn't have dared to go."

"We won't bring him out if he's a mind ter help the children have their fun," said Will; "for we know how many times he's helped us, and not such a great while ago, nuther."

"He's puttin' in for sartain, though," said Harry. "He never, since he was born, chopped at that rate for Israel Blanchard. I s'pose he thinks he's workin' for hisself, for he'll enjoy the fun as well as the young ones: they allers divide with him."

The moment school was out, the children rushed into the garrison without having counted their steps, swallowed a mouthful or two of bear-broth, and with a junk of corn bread in one hand, and pork in the other, of which they took alternate bites, made all speed for Cuthbert's; Ike Proctor dragging a sled after him by a thong of deer-skin flung over his breast, and leading under his armpits, as his hands were filled with eatables.

There they found, not indeed Scipio, for he had taken notice of the movements of Harry and the others, and returned just after them; but that which suited their purpose equally well, — a good many large logs together, with a quantity of smaller wood cut into fire-lengths.

Without a moment's hesitation they rolled a log, three feet in diameter and five in length, on to the sled, and by their united strength hauled the burden to the hearth, and rolled it, snow and all, into the fireplace. Then came a back stick half as big, and top of that a smaller one, making a true taper against the back.

The next thing in order was a forestick; for this purpose they selected a white-oak stick eight feet long and one in diameter. 'Twas too long to haul on the sled.

"How shall we git it in?" asked Sam.

"Tie the sled-string ter it, and all on us drag it," said Fred Stiefel.

"No, I'll tell you how," said Proctor. "Take three sticks just long enough ter go into the house door, and put in under it: then six of us biggest fellers can take hold on 'em, and the rest hold of the log, and we can lug it."

This they did, and succeeded in carrying the forestick to its destination.

"There ain't no andirons," said Tony. "Mr. Cuthbert's carried off his andirons."

"Our folks ain't got no andirons; rocks makes good andirons," said Archie Crawford.

They searched the stone wall round the cow-yard till they found two long flat stones, that, placed edgewise, answered the purpose admirably. Dry wood and brush were now placed between the forestick and the backlogs, and a lot of large chips that Scipio had cut piled on, the boys using their caps for baskets.

By this time the hearth and floor were pretty thickly strewn with light snow. However, Jim Grant found a broom behind the door, that had been left, and swept out the snow while the rest stripped the bark from the birch-sticks in the wood-pile, and put it under the forestick.

After contemplating their work for a moment with much satisfaction, the boys clapped their hands, shouted, and capered around the room.

"Won't that make a roar?" said Sam.

"I guess 'twill. 'Twill go right out o' the top of the chimbly," said Tony. "And we'll lay down on the hearth, and roll over, and have the goodest times; won't we, Sammy?"

"Oh! I tell you, Tony: we'll bring all our bladders down here, and blow 'em up and stretch 'em, and kick 'em too, here in this room."

When Cuthbert removed, having no other means of conveying his household goods except on pack-horses, and going where all such things could be procured, he left many articles behind that the children found most convenient for their purpose. The long settle, chairs, stools, and a table, were left. The crane still hung in the fireplace. There were wooden plates, buckets, birch-bark dishes, and wooden blocks into which the settlers were wont to put sticks of pitch-wood that they burned instead of candles. There was also a kettle and Dutch oven, the former of which he had given to Mrs. Honeywood, and the latter to Mrs. Sumerford; but they had not taken them away.

The boys had brought three axes on the sled, expecting to cut some wood, and were just about to begin when the sound of a horn was heard loud and long.

"There goes that plaguy old conch-shell. I shouldn't think 'twas schule-time so quick's this!" said Dan Mugford.

"We'll leave the axes, and come ter-night and cut some more wood," said Proctor.

"We must have some clay ter roast our tails," said Nat Holt. "Where did you git your clay, Sammy?"

"Don't you know that place in Mr. McClure's gully-pasture what trembles when you tread on it, where his cow got mired last fall?"

"Yes."

"Well, that place never freezes, not hard. If you and the rest'll cut up the wood, and git it in, me and Tony and Fred Stiefel 'll git the clay arter schule ter-night."

" Agreed."

When the afternoon school was out, and the boys were about to separate on their several errands, they met Scipio, who was driving in the cattle.

" Boys," said the black, " you's gwine hab fire in de house to-night ? "

" Yes, we be : we're goin' ter fix our clay, and blow up our bladders, and play. We're goin' ter have the biggest fire ever was," replied Ike Proctor.

" And we're goin' to cut more wood, 'cause we got ter have a fire two nights, and cause 'twill take.a lot," said Johnnie Crawford.

" Well, den, you cut de leetle sticks eber so much you mind to. Ise go wid you arter supper, cut de big wood, help you car' him in; den I play juice-harp [Jew's-harp], sing, make faces like Guinea nigga, hab good time 'long wid you."

" You're real good, Scip : we'll give you something," said Stiefel.

" Weather gwine to moderate : wind shifted sence dinner, morrow be warm day ; most like ole coon in de gully come out sun hisself, look roun', see what be gwine on: dat's de way dey do when come thaw.

"Ise shoot him: no shoot him, don' shoot partridge sartin, and we hab roast. Go 'long, you tails!"

"Oh, do, Scip!" shouted the whole band in chorus.

"Berry well: see 'bout dat if massa let me go."

After supper Scipio and the children set out, the former with his gun on his shoulder.

"Don't let's kindle the fire till we git all the wood in and the doors shut," said Sam.

It was a bright moonlight; and but little time was occupied cutting and getting in the wood, when the doors were closed, and Scip prepared to light the fire.

How do my young readers suppose he did it? Well, he did not light it with a friction-match. Scip put into the pan of the gun all the powder it would hold, laid a bunch of tow over it, and pulled the trigger. The flash of the gun set the tow ablaze in an instant, and Scip flung the blazing mass under the forestick among the birch-bark. In a few moments it was on fire, gradually working its way; till at length it caught the brush and dry wood above; and then a stream of flame shot up the throat of the great chimney, roaring and sputtering, flinging a glare of light over the room that revealed every crack in the old logs, and caused the whole party to retreat to a safe distance from the volcano.

The boys screamed and danced, and hugged Scip, and dragged the great high-backed settle to the back part of the room, to keep it from being burned up, as it was beginning to smoke.

The snow melting from the backlogs and forestick set little rivulets of water running over the stone hearth, which, as they came in contact with the hot rock, filled the room with steam for a few moments. When the fury of the flame had become subdued somewhat, the boys, stripping off their outer garments, basked in the heat, and fooled, while Scip, who was an adept at the business, made faces at them; after which they addressed themselves to the serious business of the evening.

"The children won't burn the house up, will they?" said Grant, who had just come in, having stepped out to look at the weather. The blaze was coming out of the top of the chimney; and he could see light in half a dozen places between the logs.

"They've got Scip with 'em," said Holdness, "and the roof is covered with snow: let 'em go it."

"Let 'em go it," said Nat Cuthbert: "if they don't burn it up, most like the Indians will."

The tails were now wrapped each one in its bunch of clay, and then put in the cellar that the clay might not freeze and crumble away; after which Scipio treated them to several tunes on the Jew's-harp.

They now began to inflate the bladders. Some had short pipe-stems, some goose-quills, others pieces of sumach from which the pith had been removed. These they put into the neck of the bladder, filled it with air, tied a string round, and squat it, till by stretching it became slack; then filled it again, repeating the process till it would bear no more without bursting, and was semi-transparent.

"O Archie! won't they be nice for our mothers ter put hog's fat and bear's grease in?" said Dan Mugford.

"Yes, and ter keep salves in, what they have ter put on when anybody gits wounded."

"Oh, I tell you! hear me, all on you. In the summer, when we come ter go in swimming, we'll fasten 'em on us, and they'll be fust-rate ter larn ter swim on," said Ben Wood.

"Golly, you can fasten dem to you shoulders, and float way down de stream; stay in de water long you like, all day you want to," said Scip.

"We kin fasten 'em to sticks, and make a raft what will bear us all: that'll be the goodest," said Tommy Rogers.

"Then don't let's kick 'em, 'cause we'll bust 'em; let's keep 'em good," said Sam, "and think how we're goin' ter do to-morrow night."

Leaving the boys in council, suppose we look in upon the company at the garrison, who are most of them busied some way or another.

The Widow Mugford was spinning flax in the corner of the fireplace, the rest carding wool, knitting, or sewing, the boys and girls chatting, and the men-folks either repairing snow-shoes, making moccasons, or oiling gun-locks. Holdness was repairing a pack-saddle, and Honeywood was reading. None of those employments, however, interfered with conversation; and there was a general buzz all over the room.

"For the life of me," said Mrs. Holt, as she flattened a roll of wool on the back of her cards, "I don't see what has got into my hens. I ought to have brought in fourteen eggs to-day, and I've only brought in two. I don't understand it at all."

"It's not a time of the year for hens to lay very well," said Mrs. Proctor.

"I know that of old hens; but I've got a lot of pullets that were hatched late last summer. They began to lay a fortnight ago, and laid right along; and ought to lay better'n ever now, because, since the hogs were killed, they've had scraps and bits of meat. I can't understand, neither, their dropping off all at once."

"It's the same gaet wi' mine," said Mrs. Stewart. "They're fall chickens, ilka one o' them: the gude man cuttit off the head o' ilka auld hen afore Christmas; and the pullets hae laid unco weel till twa days syne. But there's ae thing beats me a'thegither, Mrs. Holt; for, though I heard them cackling baith yestreen and this morning, I got nae egg.

"I hae ken'd one hen tell an untruth, and cackle wi' the rest when she had nae laid; but I never ken't many to. They're nae that accustomed to falsehood in Scotland, whatever they may be in this country. Sae I think they must hae laid; but I'm sair put to it to ken what has become o' the eggs."

"Perhaps it's baudrons" (cats), said Mrs. McClure.

"I dinna think we hae one amang us wad suck eggs. Gin it was simmer-time I wad ca' it a skunk."

"If it was any creature," said Mrs. Sumerford, "you'd find broken shells. I warrant 'twas Scip."

"I don't believe it was Scip this time," said Mrs. Blanchard, "for Israel whipped him for sucking eggs a fortnight since; and a whipping always keeps him from stealing at least four months."

CHAPTER VIII.

THE CHILDREN'S FEAST AND FROLIC.

THE good wives now ceased discussing the subject of hens, their attention being drawn to another topic that was somewhat abruptly introduced by Solomon Lombard, who, turning to Holdness, remarked, —

"I think of leaving you to-morrow morning. I feel that I owe my life to you and your party, and can't express the feelings that are in my heart towards all these good women who've done so much for me. I sha'n't forget your kindness as long as I'm alive. I've made up some little trifles I want the women and children to have. I wish 'twas more; but a poor man's will must go for his deed."

"Not a pin nor a needle will we take," said Holdness. "We've jest done what every man owes ter his feller-man. There's broken Jew'sharps, awls, pieces of lookin'-glass, pins and needles, enough scattered round, that we kin fix up for the children ter play with. There's not a soul in this garrison but would scorn to take the value of a sixpence from a neighbor in that manner."

"I give you thanks."

"When you git ready to start, some of us'll give you a guard to the fort."

"The boys'll do that, Mr. Holdness, — Cal and I and five or six more of us," said Harry Sumerford.

"You can't go, Harry," said Honeywood, closing his book. "You remember that you and I had a long talk together at my house, before this garrison was built. I told you then that many of the boys and children were growing up in ignorance, couldn't read nor write; and I hoped we should have a school this winter."

"Yes, sir: I remember 'bout it."

"Well, right after that came the news of Braddock's defeat. Then it was, build a garrison. The Indian war broke out, and took up all our attention: every man, boy, and even child, who could pull a trigger or lift a hatchet, was needed for defence. Watching and scouting it was and has been night and day, fighting, and burying the dead. But now the garrison's built; we've got the school started, and the children in it. And this snow is giving us a breathing-spell: how long it will last, no one knows, but at the farthest not long.

"Now, I want you to keep your promise to me, and go to school to-morrow morning; and I want the other boys to go too. There are four of you Sumerfords can't read a word, except little Sammy; and Mrs. Blanchard tells me he can read in the Bible by spelling a word now and then; and nearly all the other large boys are in the same condition."

"Oh, do, Harry!" said Mrs. Sumerford; "and you too, Enoch and Elick, do just as Mr. Honeywood wants you to."

"I will, Mr. Honeywood. I'd 'a' done it long ago, and wanted ter; but I thought I couldn't be spared."

"I know you couldn't be spared, because it was life or death with us. Part had to keep guard while the others raised bread; and there's not one of us but feel under the greatest obligations to you and your company, "The Young Defenders." But you can be spared at present; and now is your chance, or never. I'll go with Mr. Lombard, and some of the rest will go with me."

"I'll go," said Holdness.

"We'll any of us go," said Grant, "if the boys'll only go to school, and try to learn. There's but one man in this garrison that can't read nor write; and there's only two boys that can."

"We'll all go ter school," said Ned Armstrong. "Harry Sumerford's our cap'n: we'll follow him if it's into the muzzle of a cannon. I 'spect, though, 'twill come purty tough ter us boys, what's more'n half Indian, ter set all day on a bench, and study a book. I'd ruther face the savagest Indian ever I see than a schule-marm; but, if the rest kin stand it, I can. I reckon we're too old to learn much though."

"Too old!" said Holt: "what do you think of me? If my poor boy Ned was living he'd be two years older'n you, and I'm goin'.

"I'm the only man in this Run, as Grant has said, who can't read nor write. I never had any privilege when I was a youngster. I hope I love God, and I want ter be able ter read his holy word: that's the most I want ter larn ter read for. So you big boys needn't be ashamed ter go ter schule, if I ain't ashamed ter go with my own children."

"Wife, how will you take care of so many?" asked Israel Blanchard.

"David and James can take part of them off my hands."

David and James Blanchard had attended school in Vermont from childhood, the family being recent settlers at Wolf Run.

Returning to the Cuthbert house, we find the boys seated on the hearth, part of them on the ends of the forestick, the fire having burnt low, and the great forestick nearly burned off in the middle, and a glowing bed of coals on the hearth.

The plans for the morrow were all arranged with but one exception. The children were very much divided in opinion as to whether Mr. Blanchard would permit Scip to go after the coon. Some thought he would; more thought 'twas very doubtful.

"'Spose massa send me to cut browse: den I go."

"No, you can't nuther," said Sam, "'cause he'll

see you take the gun, and ax you what you goin' ter do; and like as not he'll go with you to cut browse."

"I tell you," said Will Redmond: "let's go right up to the house, and I'll coax Mrs. Honeywood. You know Mrs. Blanchard's her ma'am: she'll ax her ma'am, and she'll ax her husband, and he'll let Scip go."

This was thought worth trying; and, flinging some snow on the fire, they started, arriving just as the arrangement to furnish Lombard a guard to Raystown was concluded.

"Sammy," said Mrs. Sumerford, as the party entered the room, "look behind the chimney, and get me a candle. This one's almost burnt out; and I can't see to thread my needle by fire-light."

Sammy brought out a sliver of pitchwood, fourteen inches long, lighted the end of it at the stump of another that stuck in a block on the table, burning before his parent; and, removing the nearly exhausted sliver, put the other in its place. The settlers used tallow candles occasionally; but the fat of pine that they termed candlewood was in general use. Indeed, they could do almost any thing by firelight, except to sew and read.

"Mother, this is all there is; there ain't only this one left."

"No more candlewood! Well, there must be some got to-morrow."

Will now, with all the eloquence he was master of, preferred his suit to Mrs. Honeywood, who replied, —

"I don't know, Willie. Most any other time father would let him go if I asked him; but in the morning the large boys are going to school, and part of the men are going to see Mr. Lombard safe to the fort; and I don't much expect Scip can be spared."

"Is Mr. Blanchard goin' to the fort?"

"I don't expect he will," said Mrs. Honeywood, with a smile; for she knew well enough why that question was put.

"Will you coax him, please?"

"I'll ask him: perhaps he'll let him go."

Obliged to be contented with this reply, Will slunk back with downcast looks to his mates. But help came from an unexpected source.

After threading her needle, and sewing a few moments, Mrs. Sumerford stuck the needle in her work, and, folding her hands in her lap, said, —

"Mr. Lombard, I hope you will excuse me; but it seems to me that it is so near the Lord's Day, that you had better not think of going till Monday, and then you will have the week before you. Last Lord's Day we were all in a hurly-burly, with our people coming home from Baltimore; and next sabbath we're going to start a meeting, and we should like to have all our folks here, especially Mr. Honeywood, because we want him to read the sermon, and Mr. Blanchard to lift the tune."

"But we want your company, too, at our meeting," said Mrs. Honeywood. "There are none of us can sing as well as you, Mr. Lombard; and if you can, I think you had better tarry."

"Give up to the women, Lombard," said McClure. "What great difference will two or three days make to you?"

"I am right well contented here, ought to be, at any rate: my time ain't worth much; but I felt afraid I was putting myself on you too long."

"Not a bit of it: we've enough, thank God, for ourselves and a neighbor."

Not a word of this conversation escaped Willie Redmond, who again preferred his request.

"They ain't going away: now will you ax him?"

Mrs. Honeywood asked her father, who assented, but stipulated that Scip should have but two charges of powder, one in the gun, and one to carry, as powder was valuable, and lead too.

The boys went to bed well satisfied, for, though so much of a coward, Scip was a capital shot at any small game, and would have been equally successful in respect to a bear or a wolf could he have controlled his nerves.

A few sands before recess time, Tony exclaimed, —

"Mistress, may I leave my seat?"

"What do you want?"

"Want ter git a drink."

"Yes."

On his way to the water-pail he passed the seats of Sam, Ike, and Jim Grant, and communicated something in a whisper to Ike, as he passed, that occasioned a general buzz. Tony heard something that had not reached the ears of the mistress, nor of the other boys, — the faint report of a gun.

"Boys may go out," said Mrs. Blanchard, turning the hour-glass.

"He's shot something, I warrant," said Sam, the moment they were out of doors. "I hope 'twas a coon."

The moments of recess were occupied in discussing the probabilities whether 'twas a coon or a partridge, or neither, which some thought possible.

Just as the mistress knocked for them to come in, Mrs. Sumerford, presenting herself, said, —

"Sammy, I want you and the other boys to go at noon, and get some candlewood. I want to sew to-night, there's beans to be picked over, and some of us must iron; and we can't do it by firelight."

"Ma'am, I don't want ter: we're goin' down ter the house ter fix for our supper."

"You've got your wood all cut and carried in, and you can do the rest after school to-night."

"No, we can't, 'cause we've got to fix the table, and we want ter be here when Scip comes."

"If you go the minute school is out, you'll be back by the time Scip comes; and I'll make you something for your supper."

"What'll you make us?"

"Oh! something you all like."

"Let's go," said Ben Wood. "I know where's a fust-rate tree, only a little ways."

The moment school was out, they took axes and a hand-sled, and Ben led the way. They soon came to a great pine stub some thirty feet in height, the top having been broken off years before. It was an old settler. Many a crow had been born and died in its branches; but now there was not a limb nor a particle of bark on the time-worn trunk; and, though at one time this giant of the forest was more than five feet in diameter, the whole outside was rotten as a pear, and in some places had fallen off, revealing portions of the heart-wood, so saturated with pitch as to be of a dark yellow. Three of the boys were between the ages of fourteen and fifteen, and had been accustomed to cut brush and small wood ever since they could lift an axe.

The outside offered little resistance to their efforts. They soon reached the heart-wood, and were not long in bringing the veteran to the ground, cutting off a section five feet long, and slicing off the decayed surface. The snow was crusted: they rolled it on to the sled, and some pulling, others pushing, were making the best of their way to the garrison, when the report of a gun not far away arrested their progress in a moment.

"That's Scip: let's wait," said Mugford.

In a few moments Scip came into view, and, in response to the noisy summons of the boys, held up a coon by the hind legs; and as he came near they espied three partridges hanging from the muzzle of his musket.

"That's 'cause we was good, and got the candle-wood when we didn't want ter," said Proctor; and, re-enforced by the strength of Scip, they went home chattering and shouting. On the way they discovered that they had been working for themselves as well as for their parents; since it was plain they must have candlewood to light up their long table, which how they were to procure (to wit, the table), was a matter by no means easy of solution.

At the stockade-gate they found all the girls well snowed up.

"Where have you been?" was the first question.

"Down to Cuthbert's house."

"What arter?"

"To see whether you've got wood enough," said Maud Stewart.

"Well, ain't we got enough?" said Mat Holt.

"Oh! you've got an awful sight, and it ain't very cold neither."

"Most schule-time, Maud?" inquired Ike.

"Yes; but you've got time to git something to eat."

"Bring that log here," cried Harry, who was standing before the door of the blockhouse with an axe in his hand.

Scip hauled the sled along, and rolled off the log. Harry struck one downright blow on the end of it, burying the axe to the eye, and opening the stick so much that by putting his heel into the crack, and prying on the opposite side with the axe, it fell apart from end to end, exhaling a pungent odor of resin.

"That's the best stick of candlewood I ever did see; splits like an acorn; every bit of that'll work up. You've done well, boys."

"Aain't you goin' ter do somethin' for us 'cause we got that?" said Sammy.

"What's wantin' now?"

"Tony and I want a sled what we kin have

'twixt us for our own ter slide on: we can't haul this great bangin' one."

" Well, I'll make you a sled when I kin ; but you needn't keep teasin' me every minute, 'cause if you do I won't make it at all."

" Will you put a board on it ? "

" Yes."

It was a great affair to have a board bottom on a sled : they used to fill them with basket-stuff and moose-hide.

CHAPTER IX.

NAT TAKES A BOLD STEP.

WHEN Scipio had eaten his dinner he began to dress the coon, while Harry occupied himself in dividing the candlewood into long strips for use. The boys, casting many a longing look behind, departed slowly to school.

While Harry was preparing his candlewood, he inquired of Scipio how he happened to obtain a coon so quick at that time of year; to which the black replied that he thought he knew a tree where a coon had his den, and took an axe with him, that he might cut him out if the creature was not tempted to come out of his own free will by the warmth of the day; but, not being able to get into the woods as soon as he intended, he found that the coon had come out. He then followed his tracks, and found him drinking sap at one of the troughs that Harry and the others had left sitting under the tree they tapped, and had an excellent chance for a shot.

"How'd you find the birds so quick?"

"I drink up de sap what de coon leab; den I tink so many big birches dere, p'rhaps partridge come budding: so I hide way, keep still; bime by whole lot come, light right on one de trees what you cut; dey all scattered round, else dis chile git more."

Scipio contrived to busy himself at the woodpile till school was out, when he stopped the boys just as they were starting for the Cuthbert house, and beckoned them into the blacksmith's shop. This building was but seldom used, for the very good reason that iron was a scarce article.

"See what Ise got fur you."

Putting his hand under the bellows, Scip pulled out a birch-bark dish full of eggs. "See all dem are: roast dem in de ashes."

"We won't touch 'em: you stole 'em, and ought to be licked," said Tony.

"No, I didn't steal dem; 'tain't no hurt to take de eggs from you folks for de boys hab good time, if you no sell dem."

"Yes, 'tis: it be worser to steal from your own folks; don't it, Sammy?"

"Leetle ting like egg no 'count: hens lay 'nuff more. 'Tain't like money."

"I guess you'd think 'tis," said Sammy: "jest ask my mother. Ma'am said there was a man once, he stole a piece of chalk, and then he stole a candlestick, and then he stole a flax-comb, and arter that he got so bad he killed another man, and was hung; and she knowed his folks, ma'am did."

"An egg is a good deal more nor a pin; and my father says if you are in anybody's house, and pick up a pin, you mustn't carry it off, 'cause 'tain't yours, and if you do you'll be a thief; and a thief is just the meanest thing in the whole world," said Will Rogers.

"There's worse'n that," said Archie Crawford; "'cause, in the Commandments what we say Sunday ter father, it says you sha'n't steal; and father told me and Johnnie if anybody stoled any thing in the darkest night that ever could be, and nobody never knowed any thing about it, God Almighty would see 'em, and they would be burned up in fire and brimstone for ever and ever."

"Is it any hurt for us ter eat 'em when we didn't steal 'em?" asked Ike Proctor.

"Sartain: 'tis jist as bad when we know he stole 'em; 'cause Jake Woodbridge, afore they moved off, stole a hatchet, and sold it to Charlie Musgrove; and Mr. Musgrove gin Charlie a lickin', and made him carry it back; and father said, if we was goin' ter have thieves 'mongst us, he was glad the Woodbridges was goin' ter move off, — that is, Jake Woodbridge: Mr. Hiram Woodbridge's folks are nice people."

"God Almighty don't care what poor nigga do," said Scip. "Ise keep 'em, eat 'em all myself."

But Scip was not destined to escape so easily from these young casuists, who, in the absence of all other knowledge, had been thoroughly grounded in the doctrines of the Westminster Catechism, especially those of Scotch parentage; for many of them who couldn't read had been taught it, and also much of the Bible, by repeating after their parents.

"God Almighty cares 'bout every thing, 'cause mother read to me once how he cared 'bout a little bit of a sparrow; and I heard Mr. Cuthbert tell father that black folks was jist as good in the sight of God as we be, and that 'tain't right to buy 'em and sell 'em, and Mr. Honeywood thinks so too; and it's like that anybody what can shoot like Mr. Honeywood, and make an axe, knows. So you can't eat the eggs: you got ter put 'em where you took 'em from, jist as Charlie Musgrave did the hatchet; ain't he, boys?" said Tony.

"Yes," they cried; "and if he don't we'll tell, and Mr. Israel Blanchard'll lick him."

"I did git de eggs for you."

"We didn't ax you ter git 'em for us, didn't know nothing 'bout it. We ain't thieves," said Jim Grant.

"If I put dem back in de nests, den dey know dey wasn't dere afore, and 'quire, and find out, and I be whipped;" and Scip began to cry. That took the sympathies of the boys by storm at once; and some of them began to cry in unison.

"What fools you all be!" said Tony. "I'll put 'em back so they'll never know; think the hens stole their nests."

"Who'd they belong ter, Scip?"

"There's one dozen b'longs to Massa Stewart's wife, there's two dozen Missus Holt's, four eggs Missus McClure's, and six Sammy's mother's."

The voice of Jane Proctor was now heard calling for Ike.

"There's the gals comin': shove 'em under the belluses. We mustn't let them know it: gals allers will blab. I'll put 'em in the right place when it's dark," said Tony.

They found all the girls assembled, laden with baskets and bags, ready to set out.

"Where you been so long? we've been waiting and calling ever so long," said Louisa Holt.

The articles to be transported were placed on the sled, except some few that the girls preferred to carry; and they set out, accompanied by the whole posse of dogs and two of the bear-cubs. Bears den in winter, and remain in a half-torpid state, it is said, without eating; and these cubs in a right sharp frost would curl themselves up in the bed the children had provided for them, and refuse to stir; but when a thaw took place they would come out for a little while, and eat, but inclined to lie and sleep the greater part of the time. Great was the surprise of the boys, who all the way had been laying plans to provide a table sufficient to accommodate so large a company, when upon opening the door they found a table extending the whole length of the kitchen, with cloths on it, and plates, some of which they recognized as those left by Cuthbert, and some the property of their mothers.

The more they looked around, the greater was their astonishment. The floor had been swept, the Dutch oven and kettle scoured; shovel and tongs were beside the fireplace; a tinder-box, flint, and steel, on the mantle-shelf.

This was not all: a forestick nearly as large as the one placed there by the boys was in the fireplace; indeed, it was from the same tree, only nearer the top the next cut. The logs were but partially consumed. The girls broke the old forestick in two that was nearly burned off, placed it between the new one and the backlogs, added all the brands, piled dry wood on top, put birch-bark and pine-cones underneath ready for kindling, and proved that they needed no instruction in the matter of building fires.

"Zuckers! how'd you git that forestick in?" asked Tony.

"Somebody helped 'em," said Ike.

"No, there didn't: we tied a string to it, and hauled it in," said Nancy Crawford.

Further inquiries brought out that Cal Holdness and Enoch Sumerford had borrowed some boards that Israel Blanchard and Honeywood had sawed out to put on the roof of the smokehouse, and made the table for them, by merely placing the boards on logs of wood, and setting Cuthbert's kitchen-table at one end.

"I'm glad we axed the gals; ain't you?" whispered Sam to Tony.

"Yes, gals's fust rate: they know better'n we 'bout sich things, and their mothers 'll give 'em things what they won't give us."

"They ought ter," said the thoughtful Dan Mugford, "'cause they work, and help their mothers in the house; and we don't."

"Come, Maud," said Tony, "let's see what's in the baskets."

"You kindle the fire first," handing him the fire-works, as they were termed. They consisted of a section of the largest end of an ox-horn, the smaller extremity having a wooden bottom. In it were burnt rags, a piece of flint-stone, and an old file. Tony held the horn between his knees, and, striking the flint upon the file, the sparks caught the rags, or tinder, in a moment. He then applied a sliver of candlewood dipped in brimstone, and it kindled directly. This was the way fire was kindled in those days, and long since that. I have kindled many a fire in that way. In large towns people used to get pump-borers' chips to dip in brimstone, and make matches, because they came out of the pump-log in a round roll, and were very thin. We used to dip the whole of one end in the sulphur, and then break off a sliver as we wanted; one chip would make a great many matches.

The moment the fire blazed up, Maud opened the basket, and took out a wooden bowl full of sap sugar. Louisa Holt then opened another, and took out another larger bowl heaping full of honey in the comb. This made a great shout; but there was a greater one when Louisa took out of the same basket a potato, and held it up for inspection.

"Taters!" cried Sammy. "I didn't think they'd give us taters. How many is there?"

"There's just one apiece."

She took them out one by one, and laid them on the floor before the admiring eyes of the boys.

Potatoes were not raised to any great extent at that period in the older settlements; and they were still more rare in the new lands, as they could not well be raised till the ground was fit to plough.

It was now Maud's turn, who produced the coon finely dressed, one lump of fat, and then the partridges with the feathers all on, only drawn, and their heads and legs cut off.

"I nebber see fatter coon nor dat," said Scip.

Nancy Crawford was keeping watchful supervision over another basket, into which Sammy had long been trying to peep, but without success. The cover was now removed, and discovered a good-sized loaf of flour bread, and a lump of butter.

To comprehend the joy to which this gave rise among the children, our young readers must recollect, that though the settlers could raise wheat in large quantities on their new and strong soil, yet it was but seldom they saw any wheat flour, as they had no mill to grind it. Before the war broke out, they used to pound the greater part of their corn, it was so great a distance to any mill that ground corn even; and, as for wheat, it was only when they went twice in a year to the older settlements with their produce, that they got a little wheat ground; but now that was out of the question.

The corn they could pound, parch, and, when it was green, grate it; but the wheat they could not: they used to boil it.

Mothers are about alike, the world over. These good women had each a small quantity of flour that she had been saving a long time; and each of them contributed a little of her store, and made this loaf and something else that will come to light by and by.

"What's in that Indian basket?" said Sammy: "must be something nice, 'cause you keep it till the last. Ma'am said if we got the candlewood she'd give us something we'd like; and we got the best candlewood ever was, or ever will be."

Alice Grant took the cover from the basket, and exposed to view a heap of doughnuts.

"There's one apiece and one over," said Alice.

"We'll give that to Scip, 'cause he got the coon and the birds," said Tony.

"Flour doughnuts fried in the new hog's fat: I didn't think ma'am would give us them. Ain't my ma'am good, Tony?"

"I think all our ma'ams are the best ma'ams ever was," said Mugford.

"Mother was going to make a great custard-pie, and I was going to help her make it; but the hens they've stopped laying," said Maud Stewart.

The boys, at this, interchanged glances, but made no remark.

"Who's going to do the cooking, — boys, or girls?" said Jane Proctor.

"We're goin' ter cook the tails, Scip's goin' ter cook the birds; and we want you ter cook the coon and taters, and make the tea," said Nat Holt.

Perhaps our young readers will wonder where the tea came from. Well, it was not raised in China, but was mountain mint, and grew on the hills. It was drank at meals when a change from milk, bean-broth, and porridge, was desirable. Beer and rye-coffee were also common; "bought-en" tea and coffee, only on great occasions, and at present they were not thought of.

The girls commenced operations first. They made the tea in a teakettle, boiled the potatoes in a kettle left by Cuthbert, and baked the coon in the Dutch oven, setting it on some coals in a corner of the fireplace, and then putting live coals on the cover. The Dutch oven was a great affair in those days, and until cookstoves came into use.

The whole front of the hearth was left clear for the boys and Scip, who lost no time in improving the opportunity; the girls only using the crane, and one corner for the Dutch oven.

There was a large quantity of hot ashes, the result of the former fire, and plenty of coals from the old brands. The mass was raked open, the hearth swept clean, and the lumps of clay containing the tails placed on it.

It was now Scip's turn. He mixed some clay in a pail with water to the consistence of thick cream, and, plunging the birds one by one into the composition, let them remain a few moments till the feathers were wet and thoroughly saturated with the mixture, and then, holding the bird before the fire till the clay was partially dried, repeated the operation. When they were all well coated with it, they were placed on the hearth with the tails, and the whole immediately covered up in hot coals and ashes, the hearth also being hot below.

The greater portion of both boys and girls were now employed in setting the table. In the middle and at each end were blocks in which were stuck long slivers of candlewood, and two more on the mantle-shelf. These were not to be lighted till they sat down, as they made a good deal of smoke.

Indeed, there was not the least need of more than one, as the huge fire gave light enough; but the boys thought they made a grand show, and so they did.

The girls had not the least difficulty in knowing when the potatoes were done, as they could try them by sticking in a fork; but Scip, from long experience and without experiment, was able to do the same in respect to the birds and the tails.

Uncovering the birds, he gave one of them a thump on the hearth to break the clay, opened it, and took out the partridge as you would take a chestnut from the burr; feathers, down, and pin-feathers all came off with the clay stuck fast in it, for it was nearly the hardness of brick.

"Dere, you chillen, what you say to dat?" said Scip, holding up the bird by the string tied to its legs. "Yah, yah, yah!"

"What you say ter that?" shouted Tony, holding up an appendage he had just taken from the clay.

" I say ebery ting be most fust rate."

The potatoes were so mealy it was difficult to pare them; and there was no lack of gravy, for the Dutch oven was half full of coon-grease, which will not surprise those of my readers who have seen a right fat coon with his jacket off.

The candles were now lighted, Scip carved, and then all sat down together, without distinction of color; indeed, each one wanted to sit next to Scip, who had covered himself with glory.

There was no quarrelling, no fault-finding, but plenty of laughing and talking. They helped themselves and each other, three or four drinking out of one mug passed from hand to hand, for dishes were not in excess; Tony and Sam, Jim Grant and Ike Proctor, eating out of the same plates: they were, however, wooden trenchers, square, and of large size.

The children, proceeding in a manner quite different from that which grown-up people would probably have adopted, devoured the delicacies, wheaten bread, and doughnuts, in a jiffy, and then commenced an attack upon the more substantial viands.

While thus occupied, the door suddenly

opened; and they were very agreeably surprised by the arrival of Nat Cuthbert, accompanied by Prudence Holdness.

As our readers may also be somewhat surprised that none of the large boys and girls at the garrison bore them company, we will explain the matter.

Why it was that Ephraim Cuthbert took up land, and made a home for himself and family at Wolf Run, presenting the strange contrast of a Quaker household dwelling among and on the best terms with a community who with all their heart and soul believed in returning blow for blow, has been sufficiently explained in the previous volumes.

Suffice it to say, then, that Ephraim Cuthbert, though a Quaker of the straitest sect, was at the same time a fond parent, and, having buried two boys, was especially indulgent to Nat, his only surviving son.

Thus it came to pass, that while at home the lad was instructed in the peculiar principles of the Friends, whether he would hear or forbear, and occasionally went long journeys with his parents to a quarterly or yearly meeting, yet he was permitted to have a rifle to kill game; and though not allowed to attend shooting and wrestling matches, quilting-bees, and pumpkin-parings, — where the young people of both sexes (in respect to the two latter), got together in the evenings, — and was not allowed out after dark; nevertheless he went berrying, nutting, hunting, and fishing with all the boys and girls; could shoot, wrestle, run, or jump. Harry Sumerford and Ned Armstrong were the only two boys in the Run who could lay him on his back; and he could fling the tomahawk with the best.

Nat almost lived in the family of Holdnesses, between whose son George and himself there existed the strongest attachment. In consequence of these outside influences, the Quaker notions in which he had been bred became pretty thoroughly honeycombed.

When, therefore, at the beginning of the Indian outbreak, the settlers proceeded to draw the lines between resistants and non-resistants, Ephraim Cuthbert resolved at once to forsake house, lands, and crops, and remove to a community of Quakers in Bucks County, as the only method to prevent his children from becoming world's people outright. Then poor Nat discovered that he loved Prudence Holdness as his own soul, and could not live away from her, though he had never dared to tell her of it.

No marvel, therefore, that when, after nursing his passion for months among the uncongenial residents of Bucks County, and having come of age, he stumbled upon his old neighbors and playmates at Lancaster, he at once accepted the invitation to return with them: indeed, it was just what he was endeavoring to find means to accomplish.

It was, however, by no means in accordance with the wishes of Nat to become domesticated in the family of Holdness. He intended to make his home with Mrs. Sumerford; but the moment Holdness, who had a heart as big as an ox, caught sight of Nat (the second self of his dead boy), he flung his arms around him, declaring that he was his boy by every title, and, as for his going anywhere else, he'd never hear a word of it.

When they got to the Run, Mrs. Holdness was equally decided: so there was no other way left for Nat, except to yield.

He was, however, in an awkward position,

though having obtained one great object of his wishes, — a residence at the Run; for, while he knew the state of his own feelings in respect to Prudence, he was by no means certain that hers were similar in regard to him. Persons in his condition always acquire a facility of tormenting themselves.

Labor was always scarce at the Run : the girls, when work was pressing, often shared the toils of the boys, and romped with them in the intervals.

Nat was not ignorant that Prudence Holdness could paddle a canoe, handle an axe or sickle in an emergency, and shoot a coon or even a deer when the larder was empty and the men-folks away; that she was in many respects like her father in disposition, and despised the principle of non-resistance so prominent in Quakerism.

He felt quite sure, that, despite his Quaker origin, she once cherished towards him a feeling stronger than friendship; but many things had transpired that might have nipped that feeling in the bud.

There had been some alienation between Cuthbert and the other settlers, about the time of his removal. Intercourse had in a measure been broken off; and Cuthbert would not permit his children to mingle socially with those of the settlers, and went away in such haste that Nat had no opportunity for a parting interview.

The mode of living at the block-house afforded no facilities for private intercourse, unless one had got farther along, and possessed more confidence, than fell to the share of Nat.

However, he strove to be of good courage, and flattered himself that Nat Cuthbert wearing a hunting-shirt, with knife and tomahawk at his belt, with a reputation for courage under fire, evidently approved by her father, and wounded to boot, must make a very different impression upon a girl of her spirit, than the same Nat wearing a broad-brim, arrayed in Quaker garb, and who as yet had not defined his position. He at length made a confidant of Harry, who advised more boldness.

"Go at her," said Harry: "she likes you, I know she does; and gals like her, they want a feller to show some grit, stick right up ter 'em."

Harry contrived to get Cal out of the way for some days at meal-time, so that it fell to the lot of Prudence to cut Nat's meat, and dress his arm;

for Joan declared she wouldn't. At length the boy mustered courage to say to Prudence that he would like to take a look at the old spot, and invited her to go with him, and see what kind of a time the children were having, to which she assented; and thus it fell out that they were there by themselves, to the great delight of the children, who insisted upon their guests partaking of the supper. This they declined, but preferred to sit beside the fire upon the great settle, and eat bread and honey that was brought to them on a trencher.

Nat could not have been placed in a better position; for it was not difficult to find topics of conversation, in such circumstances, between old playmates.

"How natural this old kitchen seems!" said Nat. "It appears to me I can see mother sitting afore the fire; and father in that corner smoking his pipe, and every little while knocking the ashes out on the head of the andiron; little Jane on the block, the baby crawling on the hearth, and Harriet sitting on this same settle with me just as you are, watching baby. I don't know how many times I've told Cal I meant to come down here; but something always turned up to hinder."

"I should have thought you would: I should, the first thing I did."

"Well, one thing in the way was my arm's being so sore: it hurt me to walk over cradle-knolls and in a snow-path. But I'm glad I didn't; for, if I had come down here into an empty house, it would have seemed lonesome enough to what it does now before this blazing fire, and when the children are having such a tearing time."

"It seems much the same to me. I've spent many a day here with your mother and the girls. I used to help your mother draw her webs into the loom. I sha'n't forget very soon the time that our boys, Jeff McClure, Ned Armstrong, myself, and Joan came to call you and Harriet to go blueberrying on the mountain; and a bear with cubs after her stood up on her hind-legs right afore us. We girls took to our heels, never stopped till we got home; and we had been home but a few minutes when you and George came after a mule to bring the bear home, for you had killed her."

"Yes: I had one of the cubs, and Ned the other; and we kept 'em ever so long, just as Tony and these boys are doing now."

"Just think of it! three out of those six boys

are dead, all killed by the Indians in one day at Braddock's fight. And that's but a small part: think of all Mr. McDonald's family, and poor Alex we all loved so well, eleven souls all butchered in one day; and after that Mr. Crawford, Mr. Mugford, Biel Holt, and Mr. Campbell who was killed by a tree falling on him, — fifteen people killed out of this settlement in one fall and part of a winter, and all but one by the Indians."

"Well, I hope my arm 'll get well some time, and that when the next fight comes I sha'n't be disabled the first fire; for I didn't come back here to be a looker-on."

Nat had gotten thus far in defining his position, when Will Redmond, of whom all the Holdness household made a pet, came, and clambering up into Prudence's lap said, —

"We've done supper, and we're going to play blindman's-buff. Won't you and Nat play with us?"

"Nat can't play," said Prudence, "with his wounded arm: we'd better go home."

"Yes, I can: I'll lash it."

He took a sliver of candlewood, and going up garret found some flax-ropes. With these Scip lashed Nat's arm firmly to his body; and they joined the children in their sport, till a horn blown at the garrison summoned them to return; when with firebrands in their hands, to keep off the wolves who were howling just back of the house, and occasionally showing themselves, they obeyed the signal.

The moment they started, Scip pressed close to the side of Nat, holding to his hunting-shirt, while the boys mimicked the howling of the wolves, waving their firebrands, and daring them to come on.

CHAPTER X.

THE MEETING IN THE WILDERNESS.

NAT was so far from sustaining any injury in consequence of joining in the sports of the children, that he appeared in most exuberant spirits the next morning, and went off into the woods with Harry; for what purpose, no one could tell, since they took with them neither an axe to cut browse, nor a gun to kill game, and returned as empty-handed as they went.

"I wad like some one to tell me what has become o' my Maud," said Mrs. Stewart, while she was washing the breakfast dishes; "she's nae buskit [dressed] for school: ca' for her as ye gang."

In a few moments the delinquent entered the room, bent almost double.

"Eh, minnie, I hae found a whole lap-fu' o' eggs. Did ever ye see sic a sight in a' your born days?"

"I thought it might be some sic gaet [way] : I could na' believe, when I heard them keckle ilka day, that the creatures God made wad lie sae. Ane hen hae laid, and anither ane hae laid to her: I hae many times ken't them do that."

"Did na' God mak' everybody, mither?"

"Ay, all and every."

"But Sally Woodbridge lied, and her mither whipped her."

"Hout, awa' wi ye, clatterin' about your neebors. Ye maun ken that God made men upright, but they hae sought out many inventions, and done wrang; but the creatures hae done nae wrang, but staid where they were put."

"Why did na' the hens do wrang, mither?"

"Cause they could na'."

"Wish I'd been a hen: then I could na'."

"Whisht, ye silly taupie! Ye hae no right to think any sic a thing: ye maun strive wi' yoursel', and do the very best ye can, and leuk for help frae the Lord. Sit doon now, and let me kaim the feathers and straws out o' your hair; and gang to school like a good lass, as it's like ye are for the maist part. The Lord be wid ye, and haud a grip o' ye, for we are indeed like sheep amang wolves. The times are heart-breakin'; and whiles I'm fain to wish I was once mair in bonnie Scotland wi' my leetle flock."

As the mother uttered these last words, Maud felt a tear drop on her neck.

"What makes ye greet, minnie?"

"I canna' help it for thinkin' o' bygones; but dinna tell your father ye saw me greet. We're na' so strong-hearted as the men, and he's burden enough o' his ain to bear, puir man; I would na' add to it."

"Mither, ye never did see sic a place as where I fand the eggs."

"And what had ye to do, to gang afore school? and how got ye sae mony feathers and straes and sae muckle dirt on your claiths and in your hair?"

"Ye maun know, mither, there was some bundles o' lint [flax] in the hovel, and ait strae put ower them; and the hen, she squat in 'twixt two o' the bundles that were nae close togither, and pulled down the strae to make her nest. I wad never hae fand it, but I went doon on my knees, and creepit round, and howkit amang the bundles. Mrs. Holt says she has nae doubt her hens hae done likewise; and after school Tony and a' the lads be gaun to hae a look for them."

It is perhaps hardly necessary to say that the search of the boys was entirely successful.

These Scotch children when conversing with their parents made use of broad Scotch, but the moment they joined the others began to talk like them.

McClure, though in general he made little use of his native dialect, whenever he became provoked or much interested went back to that tongue in which he could express his feelings most satisfactorily to himself, in all the minute shades of meaning; and even Honeywood, though he had been so long absent from his country and kin, would, when moved, occasionally use the Devonshire *patois*.

The afternoon of Saturday was a half-holiday for the children; and after hunting for and finding the eggs, and bringing up the boards from the Cuthbert house, the children, both girls and boys, went to slide on the river, that is, on their feet. These young folks had never seen a pair of skates, although they had heard about them.

The men and older boys were variously occupied in preparing wood for the Lord's Day, putting a roof on the smokehouse, and pounding corn at a great hominy-block made to be worked by three or four strong men. Honeywood was shoeing Lombard's mules; and the rest were cutting wood in the forest, and hauling it within the stockade; and the bears, tempted to leave their beds by the mildness of the air, had clambered to the roof of the south-western flanker, and were sleeping in the sun all in a heap, their paws over each other, and their heads laid one upon the other, just like so many kittens. Harry was making a frame-sled for Tony and Sam, while his mother was spinning flaxen twine to be twisted into a rope by which to haul it. The settlers had a simple machine of their own, with which they could twist ropes from flax, tow, and hemp. They also made ropes of straw with a throw-crook, that were very useful; but for most purposes thongs of moose-hide, withes, and bark ropes were preferred, because the material was at hand, and the labor of manufacturing slight, whereas flax was scarce and of great value. But Sammy had been a good boy at school; and, since Harry was to make him and Tony a sled, the mother contributed the rope as a reward for good behavior in the past, and a stimulus to future effort in the same direction.

"I can't imagine," said Israel Blanchard as they stopped pounding corn a few moments, to take breath, "what can have become of our Seth. Franklin must have finished his forts by this time. I'm afraid something's happened to him,—that either he's sick, or the Indians have come on them in strong force, and killed both the workmen and the soldiers that guarded 'em."

"I guess not. Most likely they've had to wait for supplies of provisions, or tools for the workmen, or perhaps for soldiers. You may hear from them at Raystown, when we go to guard Lombard," said McClure.

"That's what I'm in hopes of. There's the shaft to our grist-mill, and the water-wheel we made so long ago: what a nice time it would be, if Seth was only here, to work on that while this snow lasts! I'm tired of this pounding corn: it's no better than slavery."

"If you had your gear all made, you wouldn't dare to build the mill; for the Indians know the worth of a mill ter us as well as we do ourselves; and the first time they came round they would burn it up, because we've got ter build it some ways from the garrison," said Holdness.

"True; but it's goin' to take a long time to make the running gear, and especially the stones. The Indians can't burn them up; and we might be cutting the stuff for a dam. Seth understands mill-work better'n I do. He worked on a mill in Vermont, with a man who was a reg'lar millwright. They built a saw-mill and grist-mill. The man cut himself with a broad-axe, and Seth had to finish the job; and he learned to 'space gear.' I'm determined to have something when he comes, — a hand-mill, or a horse-mill, or something different from this concern just fit to punish malefactors."

"Better have a horse-mill, then," said Proctor. "We can have that inside the stockade. I think this hominy-block is hand-mill enough."

"A horse-mill would be enough sight better; and is all the thing, ter amount ter much, we could have inside the fort," said Holdness.

"It's as much work to make the stones for that as it is for a grist-mill, and a good deal of work to make the gear; and, after it's done, it's a poor affair 'long side of a water-mill," replied Blanchard.

That night, around the fireside, they consulted

in respect to the arrangements for the morrow, and agreed upon the following plan, as the most convenient for all : —

That as all were to attend meeting, so, in order to afford the women-folks time to perform their milking and necessary work, they would have but one service of considerable length, occupying the middle of the day when it was warmest; and but two meals, dinner and supper together, after the service, and porridge, bean-broth, or milk, for the children before going to bed, if they wanted it.

It was resolved to make the singing very prominent in the service, and for these reasons, that none of them had been accustomed to take any active part in meetings except two or three of the women, and there were among them an unusual number of singers. The Blanchard family were all singers; so were the Crawfords and many others. Mrs. Sumerford and several of the other women knew both the words and tunes of old hymns that had been handed down from parents to children, and so much changed that they never would have been recognized by their authors.

They were not destitute of psalm-books. Israel

Blanchard had one volume of the New England Psalm-Book that had been in use more than a hundred years. There were among them several psalm-books, and portions of them, of different kinds, much dilapidated, yet could be used.

They, however, apprehended no difficulty on that account, as it was the custom in that day for a person appointed, to read two lines of the hymn or psalm, and then they were sung; then two more were read and sung.

Our readers must not suppose that Israel Blanchard could read music because he set the tunes and led the singing in his native place; for neither he nor his family knew a note of music: it was all singing by rote. Indeed, this was the way this part of worship was conducted all over New England. Our forefathers had such a wholesome dread of the formal religion of which they had seen so much in England, that they shrank even from the least approach to it, and chose to sing by rote in the greater portion of their churches.

This, however, by no means implies discord. Israel Blanchard possessed an accurate ear, thoroughly trained, a sweet and powerful voice, and never made a mistake, He was aided, however, in lifting the tune, by a wooden trumpet called a pitchpipe, that served the purpose of the tuning-fork now in use.

The most singular part of the matter is, how they ever managed to sing words arranged with so little attention to rhythm, and that men who, like the authors of the New England Psalm-Book, were ripe scholars, and not only familiar with the Hebrew, but the melodious flow of the Greek and Roman verse, could have written in such a style. The only possible solution seems to be, that they were so anxious to preserve not only the exact meaning, but as much as possible the very words, of the original, that they neglected smoothness of versification; which will be evident to our readers when we come to quote some of these psalms.

Many of these tunes, "Old Hundred" for instance, had been regularly composed; but neither Blanchard nor the others had ever seen the music, nor could have read it if they had, but learned the tunes by hearing them sung.

In short, they obtained their music somewhat as they did good fruit before they knew how to graft. There were some few trees of good fruit that had been brought over from England, and from these they took the sprouts: so they caught the tunes, and in both cases obtained the music and fruit.

The sabbath sun, rising over the mountains, gave promise of a delightful day; and at the appointed hour the settlers assembled for the worship of God.

It was a most singular assembly in more respects than one. There was not, as on most occasions of similar character, a gray head in the room; while children and youth predominated in numbers. It would have made a recruiting-sergeant's heart glad to have viewed that assembly of stalwart men, and youth on the verge of manhood.

There was not a small or inferior-looking person among them. They were either tall and raw-boned, or above the middle size, thick-set and compactly built. Harry Sumerford, Nat Cuthbert, and Cal Holdness were models of manly beauty, notwithstanding their rough garb, and faces bronzed by winter sun.

The men who sat in close proximity composed a formidable group. Their large and muscular frames were hardened by unremitting toil and exposure; and their countenances, even in repose, preserved an expression of stern resolve. Honeywood was the largest and altogether the most powerful man among them, and yet was so perfectly proportioned that most persons, except they were placed side by side, and some even then, perhaps would have pronounced Holdness, McClure, or Stewart larger.

Holdness was little more than six feet in his stockings, and, to one unaccustomed to judge of men, appeared much taller than Honeywood; yet there was not a quarter of an inch of difference between them even in height: while Honeywood was more compactly built, and every muscle rounded into the most perfect symmetry; he was one of those denominated, in common parlance, a deceiving man.

The assembly presented a most graphic illustration of the principle of toleration promulgated by William Penn, seeing there was a most singular admixture of tenets. Holt and his family, and that of Holdness (as far as Holdness had any religious bias), were English Methodists by descent, many of whom were scattered through the Province and also in the other colonies; and, whenever a few of them lived near each other, they were wont to meet for religious service occasionally, the remainder of the time worshipping with other sects, and sometimes joining them; but there was no Methodist society in the Province till long after the date of our tale.

The parents of Honeywood were Episcopalians. He had, however, been separated from them when a child, and since that time had lived among both Methodists and Quakers, but had never united with any body of Christians.

Nat Cuthbert, though he had abandoned the Quaker principle of non-resistance, still held to the rest of their tenets, and was what might be termed a fighting Quaker. McClure, Stewart, Grant, Armstrong, and the Crawfords, were Presbyterians.

The Blanchards and Sumerfords were Congregationalists; Proctor was a Baptist; Heinrich Stiefel was by parentage and education a Moravian; and the rest were indifferent as to belief, with the exception of Wood, who was a Massachusetts Puritan.

But these strange diversities of education and religious belief mattered very little to them. They were not disposed to make a mountain of a mole-hill: the great principles of truth they held in common, and were not concerned about minor differences.

The necessities of their position had bound them together by ties not easily sundered. The word "neighbor" was to them pregnant with meaning: it signified the man with whom you shared this world's goods, for whom you fought till the death, and he for you, and for whom and his family you kept watch as for your own; and each held his brother's life in his keeping. Cut off from every other hope and help, they looked only to God and one another. Under such circumstances and with such feelings, they had met for worship; and men who feared nothing else bowed in reverence before their Maker.

The attire of the worshippers harmonized well with their toil-worn, weather-beaten faces and stalwart forms. There was not a boot or shoe to be found on the feet of men or women save the Blanchards, who, being recent comers, had not worn out those they brought with them. The rest wore moccasons. Their garments were all home-made, of tow and a mixture of linen and wool, a portion made entirely of wool eked out with buckskin, and colored with roots and barks.

They had learned from the Indians the art of dressing skins, and also the method of coloring both them and cloth with vegetable dyes, but were far inferior to their teachers, and could by no means compete with an Indian, as the latter would not communicate the method of preparing, nor the materials of their choicest colors.

The same disregard of the ordinary formalities and distinctions of sect pervaded their worship. Holt was possessor of about half of an old book of Barton's Hymns, published in England in 1688, the remainder of the book being lost. Blanchard had an old Bay Psalm-Book, McClure an edition of Sternhold and Hopkins's Psalms, and Mrs. Sumerford part of a volume of Isaac Watts published in 1718. These they made use of alternately. Some of them had been members of churches in the places from whence they came. Honeywood, who by common consent was prevailed upon to lead their devotions, had never made any public profession of religion, but was esteemed by all a sincere Christian, and possessed the best education.

But, if the forms and external show of religion were absent, there were among them those whose purpose was sincere, and their hearts right in the sight of Him who looketh not on the outward appearance.

Honeywood entered, turned the hour-glass, and introduced the services by reading the following psalm, which, however wanting in melody of versification to the modern ear, produced no such impression at that time. We will quote the first verse: —

> "My heart doth take in hand,
>   Some godly song to sing;
> The praise that I shall show therein
>   Pertaineth to the King:
> My tongue shall be as quick
>   His honor to indite,
> As is the pen of any scribe,
>   That useth fast to write."

He then repeated the Lord's Prayer, in which all united. A chapter from the New Testament was then read; and another psalm, commencing, —

> " God's trees are full of juice, —
>   Thóse cedars many a one,
> Which he did plant for use,
>   In hilly Lebanon,

> Where birds make nests,
> The stork to her
> Takes trees of fir,
> Wherein she sits."

He then read a sermon from a book that had belonged to Mr. McDonald, who was killed by the Indians, and who had left several devotional books.

McDonald had been accustomed to hold meetings among his neighbors, being a man of singular piety, very much beloved, and of great intelligence, and an elder in the Kirk of Scotland.

Honeywood, on the other hand, though equally decided in his religious views, was as modest as he was brave and wise; and, having never united himself with any body of Christians (as, indeed, there had been no opportunity), felt somewhat embarrassed in assuming the position forced upon him by his neighbors: therefore, instead of offering prayer after the sermon, he called on Proctor, who immediately responded; after which the following psalm was sung: —

> " If any consolation
> In Christ is to be had,
> If any delectation
> In love to make us glad."

The closing verse was as follows: —

"And look not every man of you,
On his own things alone,
But on the things of others too,
And comfort every one."

Honeywood now said, —

"If any brother or sister has any thing to say before the Lord, there's liberty."

In any other assembly met for worship, the first person to respond would of course have been some professed Christian. But that was not the manner of this assembly, which was controlled by no precedents, and was a company of neighbors met to express that longing for communion with their heavenly Father, which he has placed in the heart of all his offspring, in the manner best suited to their necessities, and restrained only by those limits which their own sense of propriety and love for each other dictated. After a short pause, McClure spoke as follows: —

"Neighbors, I don't stand up among ye because I lay any claim to religion, seeing it would be a falsehood if I should, and render me worse than I am at this present, of which there's little need;

but I like this thing, and to my thinking we're doing the thing that's right. I'm not without my thoughts at times; for I was instructed in what the Almighty expects of all men, by my pains-taking parents. I dinna justify myself that I have paid sae little respect to their words, and have not taught my children what they taught me, specially the poor lad that's dead and gone; and, if some of our neighbors have a mind to do for our children and theirs what we have not had the grace to do for our ain sel's, I, for one, want to gie 'em God speed and many thanks for their pains-taking; and I'm free to say it glads me to see sae many heads o' wheat amang the tares; and sae it may be on that account we shall not be pulled up by the roots for our sins that have been many.

"I'm an auld hardened sinner, and maist like I'll git nae good myself; but I'll come here, and help the thing along, for the sake o' the little ones that are growin' up, and the lads that are near han' men. We've taught them to shoot, trap, hunt, and do all kind of work to git their living; but many of us have never told them whether they had a soul to be saved or no."

"Ye hae spoken the truth, Sandie McClure," said Stewart. "Ye hae spoken weel and wisely, and I am content it should be as ye say."

CHAPTER XI.

INFLUENCE OF THE SCHOOL.

MONDAY morning Honeywood and several others set out with Lombard for the fort; and, after the slight bustle occasioned by their departure had subsided, the garrison assumed an air of singular quiet.

There was little suggestive of desperate conflict, or of danger merely deferred, save the loopholes in the walls, and the muzzles of the cannon in the embrasures of the flankers.

Many of the men were absent with Lombard, others in the woods hunting. Israel Blanchard was getting out cogs for a mill-wheel : the children and boys were at school; and no sentinel paced the platform. Under the shelter of the south wall of the stockade, the cattle were chewing their cuds in the sun, and licking one another. The gates stood wide open; and several of the women were putting out their week's washing. Prudence and Joan Holdness were spreading a web of linen cloth on the snow to bleach; and their features had lost the anxious and careworn expression they had worn for many months.

All the hens pertaining to the community were burrowing into the sunny side of a haystack, or lying upon the hay they had scratched out to keep them from the snow, pushing out first one leg and wing, then the other, as hens are wont to do when they feel about right, and the world and its affairs move on satisfactorily with them; and Blanchard was whistling at his work.

Nat Cuthbert was making a wooden bowl, holding the crooked knife in his right hand, and the wood between his knees, and steadying the work with his left hand which he now ventured to use a little.

About four o'clock in the afternoon, the mountain-tops grew dim with mist; the sun went down behind a mass of clouds; and before midnight snow was falling fast, which served to prolong the season of security so highly prized by the settlers.

The influence of the school began now to manifest itself in the tone of daily intercourse, and the manners and conversation of the children and youth. Mrs. Blanchard was very decided in all her methods of government, carried matters with a firm hand, and was well fitted to deal with the rude spirits under her charge.

In this she was sustained by the parents, who gave their children to understand, if they were punished at school, they would be punished again when they got home. Thus there were no complaints to parents, and no interference; and every thing went on smoothly.

Mrs. Blanchard taught the boys, when they entered the schoolroom in the morning, to bow, and say "Good morning," and the girls to make their "courtesy."

Saturday forenoons they recited the catechism that most of them had been taught at home; and many of the parents came in, and recited with the children, which gave rise to considerable rivalry, the children striving to excel their parents.

At the conclusion of the catechising, they practised singing the hymns and psalms that were to be sung on the sabbath.

After the first week, when they became alive

to the importance of obtaining knowledge, the older boys had manifested unexampled diligence and interest.

They were not surfeited with study, and did not go to it as to a task, but a privilege which must end with the winter months, and might be interrupted any moment by an Indian alarm.

The change in their mode of thought was most observable in the manner in which the evenings were spent.

Aforetime, when night came, the girls were employed in spinning, carding, or sewing; and the men and boys in oiling gun-locks, running bullets, making powder-horns, axe-handles, moccasons, filling snow-shoes, playing fox and geese, jackstraws, mending pack-saddles, and in telling or listening to Indian stories or hunting and trapping adventures.

But now the children were engaged in study. There were so many of them in one room, the children somewhat noisy, and the women making more or less din by spinning and carding which must be done, that it was impossible for many of the boys, who had not been accustomed to study, to confine their attention; and they were wont in this case to go to the schoolhouse, make up a fire, and study there, — Harry, Cal, and Ned Armstrong, sometimes till twelve o'clock at night.

Harry possessed of great power of will, excellent natural abilities, and accustomed to accomplish whatever he undertook, now gave himself to study with all that ardor he had formerly manifested in respect to trapping, shooting, and mechanical employments. He soon outgrew both David and James Blanchard, — who at first were his instructors, — especially in respect to writing and arithmetic. Indeed, he seemed to learn to write almost without effort: before going to school, he would with a smut coal draw animals and birds to the life; and with bear's grease and red ochre would draw Indians, trees, and houses, on birch-bark, to amuse the children.

"What a fellow Harry Sumerford is!" said James Blanchard to David. "We've been to school about every winter since we were big enough, and part of the time in summer too; and this half-wild creature has learned more in part of a winter than we know."

"He don't have to learn like other folks: it comes right to him, just as it does to shoot or paint, make a tub, drum, or any thing the creature takes it into his head to do."

" Why, he'll do a sum different from the rule in the book, and get the answer."

There was also another motive, that operated on Harry like leaven hid in three measures of meal; to wit, the gratification he perceived his efforts gave to Honeywood, who by no means concealed his delight, and whose praises were constant incentives to exertion ; and, as he perceived the Blanchards were no longer capable of instructing Harry, he met with them from time to time himself.

While at school in Baltimore, Honeywood had studied surveying. He was one day searching among his books for some stray piece of paper, or some blank leaf that he could tear out of a book, on which to write a few lines to his old friend Jim Camelford at Baltimore.

He knew that Mr. Seth would return before long, with a guard of soldiers, and hoped to send the letter by them, to some of the forts from whence it would be forwarded to Baltimore.

While thus engaged, he threw out an old English work on surveying, elementary in its character, and adapted to the wants of those who were without a teacher, and likewise containing instructions in the principles of geometry. Harry, who had now mastered the ground principles of arithmetic, was looking on; he took up the book, and, on looking into it, was instantly seized with a strong desire to know more of it, and applied to Honeywood for some explanation of its principles; for the geometrical problems appealed equally to his love of figures, and to the mechanical instinct that was so strong within him. Honeywood was not disinclined to fan the flame that burned in the very marrow of the frontier boy; and Harry began the study with all the fervor of a first love, and the interested exertions of one who has found the very thing that meets the requirements of his nature.

The readers of Wolf Run, who remember how Harry obtained his model for a square, by folding a piece of birch-bark in a straight line, thus forming a right angle, to the utter astonishment of James Blanchard, — who, because he had enjoyed the advantages of education, considered himself vastly superior to the frontier boy who had never seen the inside of a schoolhouse, and then could neither read nor write, — will also appreciate the delight of Harry when his mind began to grasp the principles of geometry, and he found that he could measure surfaces, raise perpendiculars, and form angles and squares, without the aid of birch-bark, and, more than all, as a seaman would phrase it, had run James Blanchard and David " hull down to leeward."

It is doubtful whether we can express the feelings of Harry, and his satisfaction in pursuing the path now opened up before him, so well as by quoting his own language, used in reply to Honeywood, who, on his return from escorting Lombard, inquired how he liked surveying, and studying generally.

" Mr. Honeywood," said he, " didn't you never see breachy cattle break into a field of tall grass the last of May?"

" Indeed I have, much oftener than pleased me."

" Well, you know how they'll act, running hither and yon, biting and slattin', taking such big mouthfuls that the wads of grass fly out of one side of their mouths most as fast as they come in at the other."

" Just so."

"Well, that's the way with me. I'm so tickled, and see so much I want to learn, that I'm just as crazy as the cattle, and stirred up to the ends of my toes all the time. If I had to shoot, as I feel most of the time now, I couldn't hit the broad side of a barn, much less a squirrel's eye; and the Indians would go scot free for all the harm I could do 'em."

"That may be; but, when the cattle find there's nobody coming to drive them out, they settle down, and go to feeding regularly."

"But I know somebody'll come to drive me out. The snow's going: we shall soon have to mount guard, and scout; and then planting 'll be coming on."

"Well, you'll have made a beginning at least. Wherever you are, you can think, and, when you have a leisure hour, make the most of it. It's no small attainment, to learn to think."

The same general influence was gradually operating upon the minds of the younger portion of the boys.

A few days after the conversation narrated, the wind was blowing violently from the north, and a number of children were pitching quoits beneath the shelter of the stockade, where the sun had laid the ground bare. Tony, having pitched a quoit within a few inches of the hub, exclaimed in tones of triumph, —

"Look there, will you! I'd like ter see any one of you beat that."

"I'll do gooder'n that," said Sammy, spitting on his quoit for luck: "see if I won't."

"Tain't right ter say 'gooder,'" remarked Tony.

"What's the reason 'tain't?"

"'Cause school-ma'am says 'tain't. You must say 'better:' she said you must."

"You needn't say any thing: you said 'ter;' and 'tain't right to say 'ter,' more'n 'tis to say 'gooder:' you must say 'to,'" replied Sammy.

"Your Harry says 'ter,' old fellow: there now!"

"No, he don't: he used to did; but he don't now, only sometimes when he forgets."

"Well, I forgot: you needn't feel so big, and think nobody knows nothing but you and your folks."

"You mustn't say 'nothing:' you must say 'any thing.'"

"Well, if you don't hold your tongue, I won't play with you."

"Well, I'm goin' ter."

This slip of the would-be critic produced a universal shout, and for the time put an end to criticism among them.

In concluding this chapter, it may be well to state, that, in representing the Blanchards as coming from Vermont to the Run, we have availed ourselves of the privilege accorded to story-tellers of anticipating the progress of history in order to dispense with explanations for which at that time space was lacking.

The Blanchards indeed resided in what is now the State of Vermont; but at that period the territory was claimed both by New Hampshire and New York.

The ancestor of Israel and Seth emigrated from Northfield in Massachusetts, and took up land just beyond the Massachusetts line, near what is now Vernon in Vermont. A few years after (in 1724), Fort Dumond was erected, which fort was then supposed to be within the limits of Massachusetts.

For years the region was a thoroughfare for the St. Francis and other Indian tribes; and thus were the Blanchards from childhood inured to the perils of border-warfare.

Israel and Seth had lost friends and relations by the attacks of the savages; and though, when they left, Indian aggressions had become less frequent and sanguinary, they had by no means ceased.

CHAPTER XII.

A BEAR GOES TO SCHOOL.

NAT CUTHBERT was not the youth to suffer the slight approach to a more intimate acquaintance with the object of his affections, afforded by the merry-making of the children in the old homestead, to pass unimproved; but when he found that Prudence and Joan, through the influence of their mother, resolved to attend school, concluded that, while he was disabled, the best thing he could do would be to improve this, his last opportunity.

Thus it came about, that between the school, the meeting on the sabbath, and the meeting to sing, occasions were not wanting for increasing that intimacy now fast ripening into something more decided than mere friendship; and, it being generally understood in the garrison that the attentions of Nat were not unwelcome, either to Prudence or her parents, opportunities were thrown in their way by the elders, who were disposed to help the matter along.

Nat's arm had now become so well knit that there was no danger to be apprehended from using it.

A snow-storm, ending with rain and sleet, and succeeded by a hard frost, formed a strong crust, and produced considerable ice in the river.

Nat instantly stirred up the boys to invite all the girls to go sliding.

Great fires were built to afford light for the pastime. As the larger boys and girls monopolized all the sleds and sledges, the children resorted to pieces of birch-bark, and even took the shutters from the schoolhouse windows, to slide on.

This amusement was kept up till a thaw coming on so weakened the crust that they were obliged to desist, but not till Nat and Prudence had come to a mutual understanding; and it was now commonly reported in the garrison, that " Nat Cuthbert was staying with Prudence Holdness," the phrase in use at that time.

Honeywood and his party now returned, bringing news that the forts were all built, and that Mr. Seth would be along in a few days.

The settlers now employed themselves in hunting for coons, and trying to discover the dens of bears, but without success; they, however, obtained several deer and two beavers. The moderate weather now tempted the pet bears to leave their beds, and sun themselves in the middle of the day. They often clambered to the roof of the flankers (probably to escape being teased by the children), where they lay all in a heap, one upon the other, like so many kittens. Again, they would mount the stockade, and walk all round the garrison, stepping on the tops of the posts, as a cat will walk along a picket-fence, when the dew is on the grass, and she is unwilling to wet her feet.

One morning, about eleven o'clock, the school-house becoming too warm, Mrs. Blanchard set the door ajar. Shortly after, in walked Tony's bear, and seating himself upon the hearth looked reflectively around upon the school.

This was not an uncommon occurrence, and Mrs. Blanchard, who was busy setting copies, paid no attention to him.

At length a fire-coal, snapping on his back, began to smoke, and finally to scorch, causing him to jump and growl, and the children to titter.

The mistress now attempted to drive him out, and, setting the door wide open, ordered him to leave; the bear, however, relishing his quarters, and perhaps desirous of information, refused to go. She then struck him with her ruler, upon which the beast, in returning the blow, brought his paw down on the table with such force as to split it in halves, and send inkstands, writing-books, and even the hourglass, over the floor in different directions, the hourglass falling into a soft bed of ashes on the ample hearth.

Rising on his hind-legs, the bear instantly grappled the schoolmistress. At this turn of affairs, Ned Armstrong, who sat nearest, struck the brute on the head with a billet of wood, felling him to the floor; and Hugh Crawford seizing his hind-legs dragged him out of doors, and flung him with great force against the side of the building.

Tony, joined by all the children, screamed with might and main, and rushed out to comfort and sympathize with the bear, as though he were the only aggrieved party.

It was found upon examination, that Mrs. Blanchard had received several quite severe scratches from the claws of the bear. Harry Sumerford took an axe to kill him; but the children made such an ado, crying as though their hearts would break, declaring that he didn't mean to, and didn't know how hard he scratched, and that he wouldn't if the fire-coal hadn't burnt him, that the offence was passed over for the time.

Soon after this, a new interest arose, occasioned by the arrival of Mr. Seth, escorted by a guard of soldiers.

The children hung around his neck, and hugged and kissed him as though he were the parent of the entire community.

Though utterly lacking in some of the qualities considered most essential on the borders, Mr. Seth was very much esteemed, and deemed a most valuable member of the little community. Born on the frontiers of New England, he had gathered no hardihood from his rough nurture, and possessed neither the inclination nor skill to use weapons, or trap game.

But, on the other hand, his whole attention was given to mechanical pursuits, and he was remarkable for bodily strength, industry, and an inventive turn that had been stimulated by necessity; and while Israel Blanchard was stern and resolute, a master of weapons and woodcraft, his brother Seth was mild, patient, without resentment, and, though unmarried, exceedingly fond of children, and adored by them.

Mr. Seth made their kites, whistles, wooden guns, tomahawks, and sleds; and to him they confided all their plans and childish griefs, to him resorted in every emergency, assured either of aid or consolation.

The two Blanchards now went to work upon their mill-gear, while the rest were occupied in hunting and sugar-making. Mr. Seth first celebrated his return by making a dozen windmills for the children.

The day was warm, and the two brothers were indulging in rather a protracted nooning. A gentle breeze was blowing; and the children's windmills placed in various parts of the stockade, and on the roof of the block-house, were whirling merrily.

At length Mr. Seth, who for some moments had appeared lost in thought, suddenly roused up, and, placing his hand on his brother's shoulder, said, "Israel, do you see that consarn on the roof of the flanker going it?"

"Yes."

"Well, now, what's to hinder us from building a windmill to grind our grain?"

"Indeed, Seth, I never thought of that."

"No more should I if I hadn't seen that plaything spinning. We shouldn't think of putting up a water-mill, even if the dam was built and the gear made, because the Indians would burn it up the first thing; and we are only pleasing ourselves with planning and getting out the stuff, because we're cooped up here, and don't know what else to do with ourselves; but we could build a windmill right off, and have the use of it,— build it inside the stockade, loop-hole it, and then 'twould be another block-house; and have done with this everlasting slavery of pounding corn."

"But we've made our shafts."

"We haven't cut 'em off: they'll work in, and the stuff we've got out for cogs and trundles; every thing'll work in but the water-wheel."

A multitude of difficulties, some of them apparently insurmountable, presented themselves as they began to take the matter into serious consideration. There were millstones to be made, heavy shafts and timber to be raised many feet in height; and they had neither ropes, blocks, screws, nor any machinery except what they could make themselves.

But they were men who from boyhood had been thrown upon their own resources, accustomed to succeed in whatever they undertook, to accomplish great results with small means, and who took a rugged pride in overcoming obstacles. Besides, though Seth was inferior to his brother in fighting-qualities, he was fully his equal in respect to any effort or hardship in the way of labor; and, though it was said he shut both eyes and trembled whenever he fired a rifle, he would walk along the ridgepole of a building with the utmost coolness, or navigate a log in quick water, balancing himself with a pole.

"Well, brother," said Israel, after a pause of some length, "we've not much to do with, you may say nothing but our hands. If we only had ropes or tackle-blocks! but it must be done by main strength and stupidness."

"Well, main strength and stupidness it is, then;

for I reckon we've about as much of those two qualities amongst us as you'll generally find. If it was not war-time, we could take pack-horses, and bring ropes and blocks from Lancaster or Baltimore; and what we are to do for iron, I don't know."

It is not to be denied that they had a strong motive to stimulate their efforts; for it was an intolerable burden to pound corn in a hominy-mortar, and it was only a small portion thus pounded that would make bread: the rest was merely cracked, and served to boil and make hominy; and the Blanchards were not without hopes that they might be able to grind wheat, in which event their cup of happiness would be filled to overflowing.

After spending the greater part of the afternoon in the discussion of this interesting and absorbing subject, they resolved, before exciting the expectations of the rest, to talk the matter over with Honeywood on his return from hunting. They had the greatest confidence in his judgment as their equal in ingenuity, and moreover depended upon him as a blacksmith; not merely to do the iron-work, but to make the most of their little stock of iron that was scanty enough.

Half an hour before sundown, the hunters returned in high spirits, having killed six deer and a moose, and discovered two bear-dens in hollow trees.

While the rest were busied taking care of the game, the two brothers took Honeywood into the schoolhouse, that was warm and comfortable, and broached the matter to him, who counselled to call in Holdness, saying, —

"He is a man of wonderful resources, and most resolute in accomplishing a purpose in which he takes an interest."

"As for building the mill-tower," said Holdness, " we kin do that well enough, for we shall build it of hewn logs; and we are all narrow and broad axe men, and we can raise it a stick at a time. The Blanchards kin make all the gear. I've no doubt we kin contrive to get up the shafts; and Mr. Honeywood thinks he kin scrape together iron enough for the work."

"It is indeed not half the work to build a wind-mill that it would be to make a water-mill, 'cause there's no dam to build. But the millstones are what troubles me most. How are we ever goin' ter make the stones?"

"Holt can make them," said Honeywood: "his father was a stone-cutter, and he worked with him till he was out of his time."

"If Holt can make 'em, I can run the mill after it is built, and pick the stones," said Mr. Seth; "and so can Israel."

CHAPTER XIII.

THEY RESOLVE TO BUILD A MILL.

THAT evening, after supper was despatched, and the table out of the floor, Israel Blanchard, who was a man of more words than his brother, introduced the matter.

The proposal to build a mill met with the most enthusiastic reception.

"I believe," said Holt, "that, with the aid of the rest, I could make stones that would grind."

The women, at the risk of pinching themselves in the article of clothing, engaged to make the sails. So interested did they become in the subject, as to forget to turn the hour-glass, and discussed the matter till the cock crowed for daybreak.

The next morning they separated into divisions, to carry on the work.

Honeywood went into the shop, and, from some

steel obtained when the settlers went after salt, began to make drills, wedges, and chisels, to cut and split stone.

Holt went away alone, to look for suitable stones, and returned at noon, having found two, one twelve, the other seventeen inches in thickness. It is not necessary that the lower, or bed stone, should be as thick as the upper one, or runner.

He now began to shape the stones, assisted by Honeywood and Armstrong, who worked under his direction; and the rest went to the woods to cut timber, most of which was hauled inside the stockade as fast as it was cut; a portion, for lack of room, being hewed outside.

Harry Sumerford was now taken out of school to work with the Blanchards, on the mill-gear, on account of his capacity to handle tools.

It was a lively time inside the stockade, I can tell you, when the timber was all hauled from the woods. Axes were going, with only the intermission of meal-times, from sunrise till sunset. The children, and even the young men, became excessively restless, and were anxious to join in the work, or to look on; but, although the parents needed the help of the older boys, they would not give up the school; and after a few days the excitement died out.

When most of the timber was hauled in, and some considerable progress made in the hewing of it, Stewart and Maccoy, who were somewhat used to stone-work, joined Holt, Honeywood, and Armstrong, because the stone-work was a much slower and more laborious process than hewing and framing timber.

The sides of the mill-tower being now framed, it was built up to the height of five feet ten inches; the lower story being low, to facilitate the raising of the stones.

Windmills are generally built with eight sides, which was the form chosen by the settlers, as it rendered the timber short, and easier to handle.

When the walls were carried to the height of five feet ten inches, they laid the next course of timber jutting over a few inches, so as to leave a space all round to fire down upon an enemy approaching to break the door, or burn the building; since it was intended not only for a mill, but a fortress and a portion of the defences. Each story was loop-holed, the space inside being about twenty-two feet on the first floor; the building becoming narrower as it went up to the height of twenty-four feet, exclusive of the roof that surmounted the walls.

The wind-shaft that carried the vanes was twenty feet long, nearly two feet in diameter, having on one end of it a spur-wheel more than eight feet in circumference, working in a trundle on the head of an upright shaft connected with the upper millstone, or runner.

On the summit of the walls was to be laid a circular framework or curb of heavy timber, firmly fastened, and upon this another course exactly similar. Upon the upper course were to be placed cross-timbers to support the wind-shaft and its wheel; and upon this the roof was to be framed.

It is necessary that the vanes of a wind-mill should be placed head to the wind. In order to effect this in modern mills, the upper circle of timber that supports the wind-shaft and roof is placed on rollers or trucks, and the whole roof turned by machinery to the wind. In some mills there is a large vane attached to the roof or curb, and the whole top of the mill moves so easily on brass rollers that the wind acting upon this vane keeps the sails facing the wind without any care on the part of the miller.

But our settlers had neither trucks of wood, brass, nor iron, by the aid of which to keep their mill-sails facing the wind: yet they found a way to accomplish it. The upper surface of the permanent curb that was fastened to the top of the wall, and the under surface of the upper one that revolved upon it, were made as smooth as possible, and well greased. A long lever was then fastened to the roof, that reached to the ground; and the enormous leverage thus afforded by a stick like the mast of a small vessel enabled them easily to turn the upper curb with the roof, wind-shaft, and vanes to the wind.

The timbers of the walls were now all ready to raise, the mill-gear made, the lower story carried up five feet ten inches, the door of the lower story made and hung, the boards for the roof sawed, the timbers of the roof framed together, and even the arms that were to receive the sails had been hewed out, and tried in the mortices of the wind-shaft.

The millstones, however, were not ready; and

no more could be accomplished till this was effected.

It was a world of labor to make these stones, involving a great deal of cutting. They formed them from a bowlder that had a natural seam in it; and though they forced them apart with wedges without a great amount of toil, so as to have them present two faces, yet there was a great deal of cutting to be done.

In the first place, they were rounded by drilling holes in a circle, and splitting off the outside. The under, or bed stone, was also to be made slightly hollow, and the upper one, or runner, bulging to conform to it. A hole was to be cut in the centre of each stone, in which the spindle was to play, and by which the corn was to enter. Two holes of smaller size were also to be made in the edge of the upper stone, to receive bolts by means of which it might be lifted, and put on or taken off the spindle.

Manifold were the difficulties that met them at every turn.

In the first place, Holt had not worked on stone for many years, and had never seen a millstone made; and was obliged to study out the method of working, as he went along.

Stone-cutters, when they go to work in the morning, take with them a large number of drills and chisels sufficient to last through the whole or a greater part of the day, and which at noon or night are taken to the smith's to be sharpened. Now, these settlers had but few drills; and even those, in order to economize the steel, were made of iron and steel-pointed; and the iron end that received the blows would soon batter up, and the workman must wait till it could be repaired: thus one end or the other of his drill needed very frequent mending.

The place where the stones lay was more than a mile from the garrison; and much of Honeywood's time was spent going back and forth from his work to his shop, to sharpen drills and other tools.

There was not a proper stone-hammer among them; and they used nail-hammers, hatchets, axes, and even wooden mallets. Honeywood used his blacksmith's hand-hammer; and Armstrong, who was a very powerful man, made use of a light sledge that belonged to Honeywood.

It was great labor with their tools to cut the large holes in the centre of the stones; but more discouraging than any thing else was the fact that they were forced to cut these holes very much larger than is customary. Mill-spindles are made of iron three inches in diameter; but as they had not the iron, and therefore must use wood, and make a spindle twelve inches instead of three, the holes must be so much larger to admit it.

In order to expedite matters, and that they might get the stones within the stockade, the Blanchards, who had a capacity of turning their hands to any thing, also went to work upon the stones; and, as there were not tools sufficient for all, they relieved one another.

Honeywood remained in the shop, and one of the boys brought the tools to him as fast as they needed sharpening, till at length, to the great joy of all, the stones were finished except the furrows and some other work that could be done at the garrison; about all that would render the stones much lighter to haul having been cut away.

CHAPTER XIV.

PLUCK AND PERSEVERANCE.

THE whole force of the settlement was now summoned to haul the stones; and by means of a stage of timber rollers and levers they were raised to the floor of the mill; and Holt set to work cutting the grooves or furrows in them.

These grooves are cut perpendicular on one side, but slanting on the other, about one inch in width and three inches apart, running from the centre to the edge in radiating lines. Holt cut about thirty of these. The furrows are cut alike in both stones, as the stones lie on their backs; and thus when the runner is turned over, and put on the spindle over the lower stone, they cross each other like the blades of a pair of scissors, and cut the corn.

In time these ridges wear down, when they are

deepened with a chisel fixed on a handle, by the miller; which is called picking the stones.

Our readers will now perceive why the walls were raised no higher, and why they were so anxious to finish the stones; as it is very doubtful if they could have put them where they now were, had the walls been up, as there was an advantage in raising them from the outside.

Scarcely had the settlers drawn a long breath, and finished congratulating each other upon their success in this long and laborious task, than another necessity presented itself, destined to tax still further the inventive powers of the frontier's men.

Here is the wind-shaft, to which the vanes are fastened, two feet nearly in diameter, made of oak, with a wheel attached to it more than eight feet across, which must be raised to the top of the mill-tower.

It could be readily done in an old settlement where there are ropes, blocks, and other mechanical appliances; but how are men destitute of all these aids to manage with this most unwieldy affair, and to raise it twenty-four feet from the ground?

The cogs of this wheel were inserted in the side of the rim. The first movement was to build a stage of timber, one end of which rested upon the ground, and the other upon the top of the wall; and, as the ascent was sharp, a shorter one resting upon the first stage. They next fastened uprights to the opposite wall of the mill, and rising five feet above it. To these they secured ropes of bark, which they passed round the shaft, and brought the ends back to the men who stood upon the second floor, forming what seamen call a parbuckle.

Part then took hold of the ends of the shaft in order to keep the wheel on its edge. Some hauled on the ropes; others put their shoulders to the wheel itself, or took hold of the cogs; and when Israel Blanchard gave the word it went along as rapidly as the men behind the wheel could walk up the inclined plane, and was safely landed with the millstones on the floor.

"There's nothing like main strength and a leetle calculation," shouted Israel greatly delighted; and, giving his cap a spin in the air, it landed squarely on the top of one of the pickets of the stockade.

"You couldn't do that agin,' if you should try your lifetime," said McClure.

"Wouldn't undertake" —

The rest of the sentence was drowned in the shouts of the children and boys, who, coming from school, swarmed up the walls in all directions to behold and congratulate.

"It lacks but half an hour to dinner-time: don't let us be too selfish," said Uncle Seth, sitting down. "We've got along wonderful: God is good."

All with one consent sat down to rest, and receive the congratulations of the children, while the women, attracted by the shouts, came to the doors and windows.

"How are you ever going to get that awful, awful great wheel way up top?" said Ned Armstrong. "You can't, — no, never."

"The wheel's the best part of it," said Harry.

"You're right there, Harry," replied Israel Blanchard.

"Strange how quick that boy, who was born and brought up in the woods, and seemed one while to be more like an Indian than a human being, sees right into any mechanical work."

All the material was now within the fortress, and the millstones made; therefore, having thus far met with such good success, they devoted a longer time than usual to eating, and engaged in lively conversation during the meal.

"I must begin to scour up the Dutch oven Mrs. Cuthbert gave me when she went away," said Mrs. Honeywood; "for I shall soon want to bake flour biscuit."

"You may do that, wife," said Honeywood, "for you will certainly need it."

"But do you really think, Mr. Seth, that you will ever be able to grind wheat in that mill? We can raise all the wheat we want; but we've no way to cook it except to boil, or roast it to make coffee."

"Indeed I can, Mrs. Honeywood, grind corn, wheat, oats, rye, or barley. The flour will not of course be quite so nice as though the stones were fitted and kept entirely for wheat; but I can make good fine wheat flour,—good enough for any man to eat."

"Come, neighbors, we're well rested and well fed: now for a hot afternoon's work."

The wind-shaft was much shorter than the

width of the mill at the present height; and when the wheel was set on its edge, and the shaft brought to a level, the under side of the latter was a little more than four feet above the mill walls.

Confining it in this position, they built under it three courses of timber, which brought the wall to within eight inches of the shaft and wheel; and upon these the shaft was moved from one part of the work to the other, as they wished to lay timbers: thus, as the wall grew, the shaft and wheel went up with it.

In this manner the wall was built, the stationary curb put on, the movable curb upon that; and when both were finished there stood the wheel and shaft in all their glory, supported by the two round sticks upon the upper curb; and the children, brimming over with excitement and anticipation of flour biscuit and sweet-cake, amused themselves by shooting arrows at the rim of the wheel. The surfaces of the curbs where they rested upon each other were made perfectly smooth, and smeared with tallow; oblong holes were likewise made in the movable curb, in which tallow could be placed, and oil poured, that would lubricate the surfaces of both. Upon this movable curb the whole head of the mill, containing the great wheel, its shaft, and the vanes, was now to be built, so that by the revolving of this upon the lower one, the vanes could be turned to the wind.

They next proceeded to form the head of the mill. Two beams were laid parallel with the wind-shaft, and far enough apart to permit the great wheel to revolve between them; and the space on the sides floored over, thus leaving a hatch-way in the middle for the wheel and for stairs; and a loop-hole cut out for light. Two cross-beams were now fastened to the last-named parallel beams for the bearings of the wind-shaft, one not far from the middle, the other at the outside edge of the curb; and a hard, smooth stone, slightly hollowed, let into it, for the outer end of the shaft to turn on. At the other end was placed a block of seasoned rock-maple to receive the gudgeon in the end of the shaft.

This should have been made of iron; but it was absolutely necessary to hoop with iron the outer end of this shaft in which the arms were placed; and the iron could not be spared for both purposes. Mr. Seth, however, made the gudgeon of locust-wood; and, as the strain on the end of the shaft was very great, he left eighteen inches of the end square, and fitted four pieces of tough oak to it, leaving on one side a space of three inches in width across the whole side, into which he drove wedges as hard as the wood would bear.

"Nothing like *having* to do a thing," said McClure.

Another timber was fastened on the under side of the parallel beams to receive the gudgeon of the upright shaft, by which the wind-shaft was connected with the upper stone.

The roof was left uncovered till the last, for the convenience of working, and getting up timber and other things from below.

The next work in course was to place the arms on which the sails were stretched in the mortises of the wind-shaft. They were forty feet in length, and deep in proportion to their width, hewed in the form of joist, each stick running through and forming two arms, or vanes, and tapering to a few inches in diameter at the ends.

When in place they were secured by wedges; and, as they revolved, the ends approached within three feet of the ground.

Holes were mortised in these arms in a slanting direction, and slats put through, across the ends of which narrow strips were fastened, thus forming a lattice-work to support the cloth.

These slats formed a ladder on which the miller could ascend to put on or take off the sails, or reef them if the wind was too violent.

This work was finished just as school was let out at night. The children immediately began to amuse themselves by setting the arms whirling, which, once started, would revolve for some moments.

"Uncle Seth," said Tony, dripping with sweat, from his exertions in turning the arms that he could with difficulty reach, "don't it go round like every thing?"

"Yes, my lad; and to-morrow we must make something to keep it from going round like every thing."

"What do you want to stop it for, Uncle Seth? I thought you wanted it to go like lightning."

"We want to be able to govern it. It might go so fast in a hard breeze as to set the mill on fire, or tear it all to pieces. Don't the school-ma'am have something to govern the little boys' tongues when they go too fast?"

"She has a long stick, and wales us."

"That is to keep you in the right track; and that's what we mean to do with the mill."

The next morning they began to make this governor, termed a brake.

It was made of four pieces of curved wood as wide as the rim of the great wheel, and put together in joints, that it might accommodate itself to the shape of the wheel; it was, in fact, an enormous wooden band.

This being flung over the rim of the wheel, one end was brought down, and fastened to a beam, and the other brought beneath the under side of the wheel, and attached to a great lever; one end of the lever being confined to the side of the mill. When the lever is lifted by a rope, the brake is entirely clear of the wheel that turns under it; but, when the lever is let down, this wooden chain hugs the rim of the wheel so hard, it cannot move.

The lever that was to move the head of the mill was now to be constructed.

This required a stick of timber sixty feet long,

and a foot or more in diameter, great force being necessary to move the head of the mill, as there were no trucks or rollers of any kind between the two curbs; but they worked wood to wood, though the surfaces were smooth and well greased.

It was not an easy matter to raise such a timber to so great a height without any of the ordinary appliances for such work.

While the Blanchards were making the brake, Holdness and others hewed out the lever, and split the end of it with the whip-saw, and spread the parts like a cart-tongue, thus forming a brace, and enabling them to reduce the size of the stick, which was of great importance to them.

That night the children ran to the mill as usual to enjoy their sport, but were unable to move the vanes. Calling the girls and larger boys to their assistance, they tugged with all their might; but in vain.

Archie Crawford ran into the block-house to tell Mr. Holdness that the mill wouldn't go round.

" Well, we don't want it to go round," was the reply. " Bimeby you'll break your necks ridin' on the arms. Let the mill alone."

Thus repulsed, the children betook themselves

to Uncle Seth, who, finally going out, lifted the brake, and, after lighting his pipe, sat down to smoke, watch the children lest they should injure themselves, and deliberate in respect to the method of raising the great lever to its place.

He was soon joined by his brother, and finally by Holdness and McClure.

"Neighbors," said Uncle Seth, taking off his cap, and crushing it between his hands, as he was wont to do when devising any thing, "in the wind-shaft we have a first-rate windlass, and in the vanes the hand-spikes to turn it with, power enough to take up a stick as heavy as two of this. I don't want any better purchase than the wind-shaft; and all there is to it is this, whether we can contrive to make a rope strong enough to hold the weight of it."

"I kin help you out of that," said Holdness. "McClure and I kin make the rope: we old trappers are good for that."

"What have you got to make it of?" said Honeywood. "Bark won't run this time of year, and we want every pound of flax for the sails to the mill."

"Make it of hide. We've got plenty of moose

and deer skins that were dressed to make clothing and moccasons: we'll take them. The women are going to pinch themselves for clothes to make the sails, and the men and boys must do the like to make the rope," said McClure.

CHAPTER XV.

ROPE-MAKING IN THE WOODS.

THE settlers were in the habit of using thongs of moose, deer, and wolf hide, to bind loads on the pack-saddles, and for various purposes. These were all collected, and given to Holdness and McClure. Some busied themselves in cutting the skins into narrow strips of great length, cutting them in a circle as shoestrings are cut; others went into the woods to shoot wolves and moose; and traps were set for wolves; and, as they could not wait for the slow process of removing the hair with ashes, the skins of the animals thus taken were put into troughs, and the hair removed by scalding water.

A small slit was then cut in the end of each thong; and by slipping one thong over another, and putting the end through, they were neatly joined together, and wound into balls.

While some were thus busily occupied in preparing the material for a rope upon which so much depended, Holdness and McClure were contriving a machine to twist it. Two posts were set in the ground three feet apart; a hole was bored in each near the top, with an inch-and-a-half auger, the largest in the Run, and with the burning-iron increased to two inches. A wheel was roughly made with boards of double thickness, two feet six inches in diameter. In the centre of this wheel was fastened a round spindle, tapering gradually, and seven feet in length, at the smaller end of which was a half-inch hole. The holes in the posts were greased, the spindle put through them to within two feet of the wheel, where it was prevented by linch-pins from working back and forth. This spindle could be made to whirl constantly and swiftly by putting a stiff leather strap around it with a double turn, and alternately pulling with one hand, and holding back just enough with the other to prevent the strap from slipping on the spindle. McClure now fastened the end of a ball of thongs into the hole in the end of the spindle; and Holdness, putting the strap around the spindle between the posts, set it whirling, while McClure walking backwards, rubbed down the strands as they twisted, with a rag; one of the boys carrying the ball that was rolling over and over in a basket.

When a sufficient length was made, they took it from the spindle, and spun another, till three strands were finished; when they twisted them together, and formed a rope of the strongest kind.

Great was the satisfaction expressed by all when the rope was completed; but this was somewhat moderated when they found that, not having made sufficient allowance for the shortening of the strands in twisting, it would not reach the wind-shaft by six feet.

"Poh! what's six feet?" said Holdness. "We can pry it up six feet easily enough."

The stick was raised up six feet, and blocked; one end of the rope was fastened to the prongs, and the other attached to the wind-shaft.

They had connected the vanes of the windmill by bark ropes, in order to make use of them in turning the shaft, as a man could not reach from one vane to another.

Honeywood held the turn at the shaft, the Blanchards and Harry Sumerford stood on the curb to receive it; while the rest taking hold of the arms of the mill, and the ropes that connected them and the wheel in the top of the mill, turned the shaft with ease, having so great a purchase; and up went the stick slowly but steadily amid the frantic shouts of the small people, till it was safely landed on the curb; and in the course of the day moved to its proper position, and secured.

It was a great day to the settlers, especially to the children; and Tony told Sam that he thought it was almost as good as an Indian fight, and fully equal to the hog-killing.

A shoulder similar to those on the end of an axletree was cut on the lower end of the lever, and a plank wheel fitted to it to roll it along on the ground; and they found there was no difficulty in turning the curb with it in any direction.

The roof, that had been left off in order to get up the lever, was now put on, and covered with boards and shingles, Honeywood making the nails from an old gun-barrel, part of a gun-lock, the back of an old scythe, and an iron ramrod. Many of the boards, however, were fastened with wooden pins; but he contrived to make nails enough for the shingles.

"I declare," he exclaimed, dropping his hammer in utter weariness when the last nail was made, "it's hard, up-hill work, this trying to make something out of nothing. I never would have undertaken to make shingle-nails if hemlock bark would run this time of year; but have covered the roof with bark, and fastened it with weight-poles."

Our readers may now hope that the settlers had at length overcome their difficulties, and that, after so protracted a struggle, they might meet with favorable winds and smooth water. But it now remained to connect the wind-shaft and driving-wheel with the stones; and here arose difficulties greater than any they had previously encountered.

Water-mills are run in this manner: In the middle of the lower stone is a hole about nine inches in diameter, through which passes an iron spindle, resting in a brass or iron socket, upon a large timber called a bridge-tree. This spindle is three inches in diameter; and round where it passes through the lower stone, which is stationary, the spindle is filled, or bushed, closely around with wood, and a piece of thick leather put over all. After leaving the lower stone, the spindle is square, and receives on its head an iron cross, the arms of which are very strong, and support the entire weight of the upper millstone, being let into the surface of the stone on its under side.

In water-mills, the spindle has at the lower part of it a wheel of some kind, by which it is geared to the water-wheel. But in a wind-mill the power is above and not below; and the old-time mills were arranged as follows:—

The spindle came up through a hole in the centre of the upper stone; and on the head of it was placed another piece of iron, having on the end of it a square socket that fitted over the square head of the spindle.

The other end of this iron entered a small shaft that extended to the top of the mill, having on its end a trundle that meshed into the cogs of the great wheel, and thus turned the upper stone.

This vertical shaft was not large, and could be thrown out of gear, and lifted from the socket, whenever it was necessary to take off the upper stone to pick it. One man could do it by putting a strap round the wind-shaft, and turning it.

Here was a demand for iron, that put the settlers at their wit's end. The spindle must be six feet in length and three inches thick; and the rynd, or cross, that the stone rested upon, must also be a stout piece of iron.

The lower end of the upright shaft must likewise have a strong band of iron; and they had already used up every scrap. The spindle could, indeed, be made of wood; and, in view of being obliged to do this, they had cut the holes in the stones large enough to receive a twelve-inch wooden spindle, instead of a three-inch iron one; but the rynd, the band for the shaft, and another for the wallower, *must* be made of iron.

"Oh, dear!" said Israel Blanchard to his neighbors as they reviewed the situation together: "I never did know the worth of iron till now; and, if anybody wants to know the worth of iron and steel, let 'em go into the wilderness, and undertake to build a mill, and cut the millstones."

"Oh!" said Honeywood, "if we only had some of the iron that is kicking about the barns and sheds of the folks in the old settlements!"

"Neighbors, I take you all to witness I'll never pass a blacksmith-shop again as long as I live, or a place that has iron in it, but I'll take off my hat," said Uncle Seth.

"We'll nae get iron by wishing, an' we'll nae big [build] a mill by saying Oh, dear!" said Stewart. "I'll gie up my shovel and axe."

"We might take some of the smooth-bores we captured from the Indians," said Armstrong. "but that would be using up our means of defence; and it's a great thing to have so many guns that the women can load while the men fire."

It was decided at once that this could not be thought of; for they had already, in their great need of iron, used up nearly all the guns that were worn out, and a great part of the tomahawks captured at different times from the Indians.

"I've got a file and an old spike," said Harry Sumerford: "I'll give them."

"The spike would do, Harry; but the file is steel, and must be saved for mill-picks: all we've got for mill-picks are the drills (what is left of them) with which we cut the millstones," replied Honeywood.

"I've got an iron shovel: I'll give that," said Mrs. Sumerford.

"I've got a long-handled frying-pan: you can cut the handle off of that. I think I can make out to use it if a little stub is left to put a wooden handle on," said Lucy Mugford.

"You can take the handle of my Dutch oven," said Mrs. Honeywood. "I can set it on the coals, or we can put a withe in it, and cover it with clay to keep it from burning off as the Indians do with their clay pots."

"Neighbors," said Honeywood, "if you should strip yourselves of every article of housekeeping you have got, it would not be half enough. I don't see any other way than to go on, and do what we can with the wood, and, if the mill comes to pieces every other day, keep making it over; and even that will be better than pounding corn in a mortar."

CHAPTER XVI.

HARRY'S PLAN TO GET IRON.

"I'LL tell you what ter do," cried Harry, forgetting, in the interest of the occasion, all the culture so recently obtained at school, and insensibly sliding back into the old backwoods dialect. "You'll overlook my giving my opinion afore older folks; but there's lashings of iron on Braddock's battle-ground, I tell yer, — picks and crowbars, axes, and great thick tires on the wheels of the gun-carriages, and great bangin' bolts in the axletrees as big as my wrist, and all kinds of iron and steel scattered over the ground, and the best of king's iron and steel to boot: Mr. Holdness says so. Anybody kin set the carriages afire, burn 'em up, and git the iron; and there's all kinds of blacksmith's tools, and an army forge there to cut the tires up with, or flatten 'em together so as ter carry 'em: Mr. Holdness said so. Now, what I'm comin' at is this ere: instead of takin' every mother's old kettle-bail and frying-pan-handle, that it most breaks their hearts to part with, if the boys'll foller me what have follered me afore, the 'Young Defenders' I mean, I'll head a party ter take pack-horses and rations, fight our way to Braddock's field and back, and git all the iron and steel we want for the mill, and farming-tools to boot."

"God bless you! the shoes on the dead horses' feet are as thick as cranberries in a swamp, — enough to shoe our horses this ten years. I'd ruther fight *Indians* than *pound corn*, any day."

"We'll go," shouted Nat Cuthbert, and the whole company of Defenders familiar to many of our readers. "Hurrah for Braddock's and the mill-spindle!"

"You shall not do it," exclaimed Mrs. Holdness. "I have two dear boys lying in bloody graves on that field; and I'll not send Cal, the only one left, to lie beside them."

"You shall not go, Harry," said Mrs. Sumerford, the tears streaming down her cheeks. "I have a dear husband lying on that terrible field, and I lay the commands of a widowed mother upon you. There shall not any of you go: there's no such great necessity. We women-folks'll pound the corn ourselves first. I was willing you should risk your life in the *common* defence, and to go after salt that we must have or starve; but I am not willing you should risk it in this manner, though it would be a great blessing to have a mill. I do wish you would think more of your life for your poor mother's sake, if for nothing else."

"You're a noble fellow, Harry Sumerford," said Israel Blanchard; "but the thing you volunteer to do, I'll never permit. Neighbors, I'll find the iron; and I take shame to myself that I've permitted this thing to go on as long as it has."

"Where will you get it?" asked Holt.

"I've got it. When I started to come here I started with my own team, came with wheels as long as I could find any road, and then put pack-saddles on my horses, and came through. When I had been here a while, I sent Mr. Honeywood to tear the wagon to pieces, and bring the iron-work, because I could make the wood-work of another wagon any time."

"I had forgotten all about it but I recall it now since you bring it up."

"I hoped when I came here 'twould not be long afore we should have a wagon-road to Smithtown, and the wagon would be a common benefit to get our truck to market."

"It would have been a great thing, Israel," said Armstrong.

"For that reason I've kept the wheel-tires, bolts, and bands of the hubs, that are very heavy, and other iron-work, though I spared some for the schoolhouse. But that wasn't all. I loved to look at those irons; it seemed to bring everything back; and I thought if I ever made a body for them it would seem so like old times at home. But I don't see much prospect of a wagon-road, at least in my lifetime. A mill to grind our corn and grain is worth more than a road years ahead. I cannot see Harry and the rest risk their lives, and my neighbors giving up the things they absolutely need, — I can't do that: so there's the iron, and Mr. Honeywood can work it up in any way he thinks best."

"Father Blanchard," cried Honeywood, overjoyed, "we're all right now, for the spindle can be made of wood, and when it wears out we can make another; and probably we can get along with only a part of the iron. I think with the tires, hubs, hoops of the forward wheels, the rocker-bolt, some smaller bolts, two gun-barrels that are used up, and the iron on the forward axletree and rocker, we can get along. I don't see now that we need take any more; and you may live to ride in your wagon yet, Mr. Blanchard, perhaps go to Philadelphia in it. Stranger things have happened."

"If that's the case," said Uncle Seth, "I'll make a wheel to suit one of the hind tires, and put the boxes in it, and we'll put it on the end of the lever instead of the plank-wheel; and there will be one wheel all ready made when brother wants to start for Philadelphia. 'Pears to me I can see him now setting up on his wagon with his bags of wheat, hams, packs of fur, maple-sugar, and potash, just ready to start, and the neighbors all giving him their errands, and can hear him crack his whip over the heads of the leaders."

That night the community went to bed in excellent humor; and the next morning the Blanchards went to work to make the spindle, and Honeywood to prepare the iron-work.

The large boys now left school, some to work on the mill, the rest into the woods to hunt, and make maple-sugar for the community, as all the men were in some way at work on the mill, which it was necessary to hasten along.

The spindle was now made, and the bridge-tree by which it could be lifted and the upper stone with it, and set to grind coarse or fine corn, wheat, or oats. The hoop that encircled the stones, the hopper to hold the corn, the shoe to conduct it to the hole in the stone, the chest to hold the meal, and the spout to carry it, were all made ready to be put together, and the upright shaft that connected the upper stone with the driving-wheel.

In proportion as the work went on, there was generated a sort of feverish anxiety in the minds of the women and children: they were constantly fearing that some new and insurmountable obstacle would arise, and could hardly believe that they should, after all, have a mill, as Mrs. Sumerford said, "right at their back doors."

The time at length arrived, when the great stone that lay on its back upon the floor must be turned over, and placed on the cross of the spindle, or "rynd."

This is accomplished by different methods. In some mills, a wooden crane swings over the middle of the bed-stone, on the end of which is a powerful iron screw that is attached to an iron bail that is temporarily fastened to the stone by two iron bolts that enter its edge: by turning the screw, the stone is lifted and held, and can be turned over on the bolts like a griddle on its bail. In some mills a tackle is attached to the crane and windlass.

The Blanchards intended to turn the stone over by hand, as the furrows were on top, place timbers on the bed-stone, and rollers on them, and work the stone on the cross by means of the rollers.

"It can be done in that way," said Honeywood. "But this stone must often be taken off, and turned over to be picked; and that is too tedious a job to go through so often: besides, it takes seven or eight to do it, and there's risk of breaking the cross and spindle."

" We must have a crane and bail, as they do in all mills, if it takes all Father Blanchard's iron."

" I think," said Mr. Seth, " yes, I know, every mite of the concern — crane, bolts, bail, and screw — can be made of wood."

As Mr. Seth said this, Tony and Sam, who were drinking in every word with anxiety depicted on their countenances, began to hug him.

"Don't be too sure, lads: 'tain't done yet."

"Zuckers! but 'twill be," cried Tony, "'cause Uncle Seth allers does what he sets out ter."

"Uncle Seth and Mr. Israel can do every thing; and we shall have the mill, won't we, Tony?"

"It can't be done without iron," said Honeywood.

"Well, Ned," replied Uncle Seth, "you've always been used to working iron; but Israel and myself have been accustomed to make wood take the place of iron as much as possible; and a great deal more can be done in that way than a man always used to having iron would think possible."

"But it's a deal of work, and will take time, Mr. Honeywood; and I don't know but the women and children and some of the men would go crazy waiting. This is a new stone, and, with the little grinding we shall do, won't need to be taken off to be picked this three months, or even four. Let's put it on my fashion; and by the time it wants to be picked, if Israel and I don't make something to take it off, and that one man can do it with, call me a numskull."

"You're a blessing, Mr. Seth," cried Holdness. "I used ter think if a man couldn't take out a squirrel's eye with a single bullet, or take a scalp, he wasn't anybody; but I see I was a fool."

All hands now worked the runner over the bed-stone and the rollers; and, when it was over, two oak treenails were put into the holes in its edge that were opposite each other, and had been enlarged to receive a wooden pin. They then doubled a piece of the hide rope, fastened it to the pins, put a great lever under it, set a large log under the lever, lifted the stone, took out all the timber and rollers, and let it down gently on the rynd, without injury or accident.

"There," said Mr. Israel, drawing a long breath, "the child is born, and his teeth cut; and his name's Peter. Now let's sing 'Old Hundred.'" So they did.

Mr. Seth, taking hold of one of the pegs, set the stone a-going, and at the same time pulled out the peg, and as the other came along gave it another whirl. Round and round went the great stone before the admiring gaze of the patient laborers, who had now brought their work so near to a successful completion.

The children who had left the mill now made their appearance, dragging their mothers by the hand.

"We will soon see whether our gear will work," said Israel Blanchard.

The upright shaft was placed on the spindle-head, and the trundle on its upper end thrown into gear with the great wheel.

Honeywood and Holdness went outside, and, taking hold of the arms, the stone that had stopped in its revolutions began to turn again.

"I'd rather grind corn in this way," said Holdness, "than pound it, if we never have any sails."

"So had I," replied Honeywood. "It is not half so hard work; and we could make better meal, and four times as fast."

"Now, girls," said Mr. Seth, "you see the gear is all right. All that's lacking is the sails; and, when you bring them on, we shall soon know whether we are done with the hominy-block."

"Well," said Mrs. Sumerford, "by to-morrow night every inch of cloth we could make by pinching, paring, and hard work, will be wove and ready."

The hoop, hopper, and other woodwork around

the stones, having been already prepared, were soon put in place, and all the bearings smeared with grease.

An estimate now being made, it was found that the cloth, after all the effort that had been made, fell short a little.

In this exigency they sawed out some boards very thin, and, reducing them still more by planing, fastened one of them, a foot in width, to each arm, and thus supplied the deficiency.

CHAPTER XVII.

THE LONG-EXPECTED HOUR.

IT was near the middle of Saturday afternoon; the boards were all secured to the lattice-work, the stone was balanced on the rynd, the women had almost finished sewing on the sails, and all were eagerly looking forward to the next week when the mill was to be put in operation, when the unwelcome discovery was made that there was not meal enough in the garrison to last over the sabbath.

There were blank faces at this announcement, especially among the boys.

"I won't pound another kernel of corn till I see whether the mill will go," said Holdness. "I'll go without one or two days first; and I'm sure I won't make the boys do it. Boil some corn, can't you? and hull it; and we'll live on hulled corn and milk. I don't believe I could lift the pestle if I tried."

The words of Holdness found a response in every breast, as was indicated by a murmur of assent.

"But there's one thing I'm ready ter do," he continued, — "shell up a lot of corn to grind in the mill Monday."

"That's the talk: I go in for that," said Nat Cuthbert. "Fetch on your frying-pan handles, old scythes, pod augers, tubs, and troughs. We boys'll shell the corn. The men-folks have done enough: they can have the rest of the afternoon."

"I say, boys," cried Cal, "let's shell it in the mill: then 'twill be there."

Some ran with baskets for corn, others brought tubs and trough to shell it into; and in a few moments half of them were astride of scythes, pod augers, frying-pan-handles, kitchen shovels, or of any piece of iron that had a sharp edge; and some shelled by rubbing an ear and a cob together.

There was a perfect storm of cobs, many of which they flung at each other.

By supper-time half a dozen bushels were shelled, the cobs picked up, and the mill swept out. The settlers, worn and weary with the labors of the last month, gladly laid aside their tools, and prepared for the rest of the sabbath.

There is an end to every thing, a moment when a watched pot boils; and thus all those obstacles of various kinds, that at one time seemed interminable, came at length to an end; and by nine of the clock on Monday morning the sails were spread on the arms of the mill; and now there was nothing lacking but wind, which was as much longed for by the older members of the community as by the children, however much they strove to conceal it under an air of unconcern.

The men pretended to busy themselves about one thing and another, and the women continued their indoor avocations; but frequent glances of the men at the horizon, and the numerous heads that every now and then popped from the doors and windows, gave telltale evidence that their minds were not on their work.

But the children, who were hampered by no such proprieties, and whose feelings gushed without control, were perched on the roofs and pickets of the stockade, watching the clouds and the toy windmills that were stuck on the walls, some of them holding up feathers to see if there was any wind, and all looking and longing.

One of the arms was fastened to the corner of the mill with a bark rope; and the end of it was within three feet of the ground. Sam, Archie Crawford, Jim Grant, and Bob Holt were beating it with sticks, and alternately coaxing it to go, and pounding it for non-compliance.

The weather, however, remained provokingly calm; the surface of the river, except in the quick water, was smooth as glass; not a branch moved in the forest; and the mill stood in the midst like a great giant, and seemed incapable of motion.

Noon came, but brought no wind.

"It wouldn't be at all strange," said Holdness as they were seated at the dinner-table, "if it should hold calm all day; for the wind has blown quite hard for the last three days."

He was interrupted by Tony, and Archie Crawford, who came rushing in to say, "There is a wind, for it has blown Sam Sumerford's feather."

The children had raised so many false alarms, that no attention was paid to the assertion.

In a few moments Ike Proctor shouted in at the door, that they could see the tops of the trees move on Red Mountain. But even this inspired no confidence; nor even the still more clamorous declarations, a few minutes later, that Fred Stiefel's windmill was going round.

"I've no doubt of it," said Honeywood. "I suppose he's turning it with his fingers."

A slight clattering was now distinctly heard by every one.

"Will you believe now, all on you?" shouted the children in unison.

Mr. Seth had made Fred a windmill, the arms of which, as they turned, just touched a piece of shingle, thus keeping up a continual clatter.

The table was vacated in an instant, and all the inmates of the garrison stood bareheaded, gazing skyward. Some light clouds were rising in the west; the tops of the trees on the summits of the hills were slightly agitated; and the breeze soon began to lift their locks as they stood uncovered.

"It takes considerable wind to move the trees when there are no leaves on 'em. We're goin' ter have a fresh breeze: upon my word, I didn't think it," said Holdness. As he spoke, a stronger puff sent the door of the garrison to.

"Why don't you set her a-going?" shouted a

dozen voices; "only see what a breeze there is."

"Because," said Holt, "there is not half enough: it takes a good bit of wind to make a windmill do its best. We want the wind to get steady, and not to make a botch of it the first going-off. There are other things: the corn is hard and dry this time of year; the gear is all new and stiff, and won't turn so easy as it will after it has run a spell, got worn, and well soaked with grease. But we'll turn the arms to the wind, and get ready."

The bark rope that held one of the arms was untied, and the head of the mill turned to the wind; and the sails began to flutter on the lattice-work.

The transient puffs increased both in frequency and strength, till the wind became strong and steady as could be desired.

Though Holt had made the millstones, as being accustomed to work on stone, yet the Blanchards were all the ones capable of running and taking care of the mill, having been used to it at home; and could also pick the stones, and therefore now assumed charge of the mill.

"Tony," said Mr. Seth, "tell your ma'am and the rest of the women-folks we are going to start the mill."

Every male inmate of the garrison was already on the spot.

With a joyful yell, the lad ran to carry the news.

Mrs. Proctor came running, wiping her hands on her apron (she had just taken them from the dish-water); Mrs. Stewart with a flat-iron in her hand, she had forgotten to put down; Mrs. Honeywood with her back hair hanging about her neck, and the comb in her hand; Lucy Mugford in her stocking-feet; Mrs. Blanchard with her knitting-work in her hands, and the ball of yarn that she had quite forgotten rolling on the ground after her, and two kittens playing with it, and striving which should have it. Yarn, too, was a precious article among the settlers.

Indeed, you would have thought it an Indian alarm, and that they were fleeing for their lives.

Mr. Seth took hold of the rope that lifted the brake-lever, while Israel stood by the stones.

You might have heard a pin drop, while every eye was noting the motions of the two Blanchards.

"Let her go," said Israel.

"Let her rip," screamed Tony, unable to hold in any longer.

Mr. Seth lifted the brake. There was a jar and great creaking, and the mill trembled; the children ran out of doors, thinking it was coming down about their ears, but when recalled by Mr. Seth came back.

The stone now began to move at first slowly, but, after a few revolutions, with great velocity.

"Put a half-bushel of corn into the hopper, Israel," said Mr. Seth.

The children were now in a dilemma: they all wanted to see the corn go into the mill, and also to see the meal come out, and to see it for the first time; but as the corn went in up stairs, and the meal came out down stairs, this was not possible: therefore they had to choose between the two.

There was not much time for deliberation. Ike Proctor, Jim Grant, Sam Sumerford, and others ran below; Tony and the rest remained above. Blanchard threw the corn into the hopper. A universal screech of "I saw the first corn go in," rose from the whole group, who, down on their knees on the covering-board, were peeping under the shoe to see the corn drop.

In a few moments shouts of, "I saw the first meal come out!" "Oh, how warm it is!" resounded from the lower floor; and then began a general stampede, those below rushing up stairs to see the corn go into the mill, and those above running down to see the meal come out.

All went down now to look at the meal: it was somewhat coarse, between meal and cracked corn, but, as a whole, greatly superior to that made in the hominy-block.

"We've got corn enough," said Mr. Seth: "we'll give this to the fowl. Very likely there's some grit in it from the new stones: don't expect we could sweep it all off, but they are clean now. Suppose we turn up a couple of bushels, set the stone down to grind fine, get the hourglass, and see how long it takes: we can guess pretty near by the hourglass."

The hour-glass was brought, and the corn poured into the hopper. The wind was strong and steady; and the meal began to pour in a steady stream into a trough that was set to catch it.

"Bless the Lord that I've lived to see this day!" cried Mrs. Sumerford, with clasped hands and uplifted eyes.

The children thrust their hands up the spout, that the meal might fall on their bare arms, crying, —

"Oh, how hot it is! how nice it feels!"

"Get away from that trough," said Holdness. "Who do you s'pose is goin' ter eat that meal after your hands have been in it?"

"Dinna fash the weans," said Stewart. "It's a day of muckle gladness: let them get into it all over an' they like. I dinna ken but we ought to pur it out before the Lord for a freewill offering for a' his goodness. Our forbears wad hae done sae lang syne, and we'll give this grist to the cattle."

"The Lord hae a grip o' us!" cried Mrs. Stewart. "Is the mill on fire?"

It was filled with smoke, the cause of which was soon discovered.

The moment Harry Sumerford saw that the mill was a success, he rolled the hominy-block into the middle of the yard, cut the pestle from the sweep, took an axe and cut down the post that supported the sweep, piled them on the hominy-block, then flung on some brush, and set it on fire; and then with Ned Armstrong, Nat Cuthbert, Cal Holdness, and some others, danced round it.

"Don't, Harry! what in the world are you doing?" said Holdness, rushing out.

"I said when the Blanchards were talking about building a mill, that, if ever sich a thing did happen, I'd burn up the old hominy-block, and dance round it; and I'm a-doin' it."

"And we said we'd keep him company," said Ned, "and we're a-doin' it."

"I wouldn't burn it," said Holdness, "because the mill might be burnt up, or get out of order, and we might be glad to fall back on the old block; or we might want to pound salt, and it would be a right good thing to supple skins on."

Thus the hominy-block, after a good scorching, was pulled out of the fire.

When the corn was ground, it was the general opinion, judging by the quantity of sand remaining in the glass, that it had taken fifteen minutes.

"Two bushels of corn in fifteen minutes!" exclaimed Mrs. Sumerford. "What an awful while it would have taken to pound it! and then 'twould have been coarse as peas, half on it."

The stones were now brought nearer together; and the meal came out so fine that Goody Proctor declared her cup of happiness was brimfull.

"If it's full now," said Holt, "'twill soon run over, for I kalkulate to grind some wheat next."

The stones were altered again, the mill made to feed slower, and a little wheat put into the hopper. The first run, being somewhat mixed with meal, was put by itself; but, when the stones were clean, two bushels were turned up, and the fine white flour greeted the longing eyes of the settlers.

"Wad I ever hae thocht, or wad I hae ever believed, had it been tauld me in my ain countree," said Mrs. Stewart, "that I wad greet [cry] for vera gladness to see the flour rin frae a mill! Ah, we dinna ken the worth o' things till we're deprived o' them, an' we dinna value mercies till they are taken frae us."

"Well Neighbor Stiefel," said Israel Blanchard, "you've lived all your young days among windmills: now what do you think of this?"

"I do say dat ish von goot mill,— goot as mine people have at home."

CHAPTER XVIII.

INDIANS STRUCK WITH PANIC.

WHILE the settlers had been so intensely occupied, spring had come; and with its advent their anxieties in regard to Indians revived, and precautions long disused were again resorted to.

It may, however, well be doubted whether the change, with all its fatigue and dangers, was to those resolute spirits altogether unwelcome.

Harry Sumerford doubtless expressed the feelings of most, when, while taking his rifle from the brackets, he said to Ned Armstrong, —

"I tell you what it is, Ned, it seems kind of good to put a rifle to your face, and feel the trigger in your hand, once more."

The question now to be settled was, whether they should remain in garrison, the men going to their work in the morning, and returning at night;

or remove to their own houses, which were loopholed and capable of defence.

The most singular feature of the affair was, that the women to a unit were in favor of going, while many of the men thought the women and children had better remain in the fort. "I don't see," said Mrs. Sumerford, "how we can stay in this block-house in hot weather. It is built of timber, and as tight as a churn; not a crack anywhere. The loop-holes are small: so are the windows, and but few of them. The cows are calving; and what to do with our milk and butter, no mortal can tell; and so many children cooped up here, 'twill be dreadful."

"That's true enough," said McClure; "but, if you go out, when in the fields we not only have to look out for our own lives, but are in constant anxiety about our families; whereas, if you stay in the fort, we are clear of that burden."

It was finally decided to remove, but that a small guard should be kept in the fort, to which they might retreat on the least alarm.

"It is high time," said Honeywood, "that these children should be put through their exercise, and practised in shooting: they have had no practice for months, because we've not had powder or lead to spare for it."

" We must have a stock of powder, and that directly."

" Indeed," said Israel Blanchard, " that must be seen to forthwith: we've been so taken up with the mill and the school, that we've neglected — I'd almost said the one thing needful, which is powder."

In view of possible emergencies, the children had been taught to shoot; and they, catching the spirit of their parents, had formed a company called the Screeching Catamounts, and in that capacity had done good service.

" It is a great ways to go to Gnadenhutten or to Fort Cumberland; but it is idle to think of sowing or planting without ammunition to defend ourselves while at work. I know we can get powder at Cumberland, lead at Fort Allen, and perhaps powder too," said Honeywood.

It was almost as perilous to go after the ammunition as to remain without it, since large bands of Delawares, Shawanees, and Mohicans, led by Buckshanoath, Teedyuscung, and Shinghas, were roaming the country unopposed.

Spring was fast spending, time precious; and, trusting to the strength of the fort, they determined to send two parties in different directions. The two parties started at midnight, but with an interval of three days between them.

The one bound to Fort Cumberland was the larger, the risk being considered greater, as Fort Cumberland stood alone, while Fort Allen was one of a line of fortresses placed at convenient distances for scouting between them.

Israel Blanchard was left in command at home, having with him several of the young men, together with Stewart, Holt, Woods, Maccoy, and the children, who, though of no account in a hand-to-hand fight, were no despicable antagonists behind loop-holes.

The greatest cause for anxiety, in respect to the inmates of the garrison, arose from the fact that they were but scantily supplied with ammunition; although, in dividing it, the largest portion had been allotted to those remaining at home.

For several days nothing occurred worthy of note; the settlers confining themselves closely to the garrison, and keeping vigilant watch. One morning, just before daybreak, they were alarmed by the report of a rifle, followed by a cry of agony, succeeded by the report of fire-arms, and the fearful sound of the war-whoop. Rushing from their beds, they saw flames bursting from the south flanker; and Andrew McClure, who was running, rifle in hand, to the platform, was wounded by a bullet that came through a loop-hole.

Blanchard, a cool, resolute man. detailed Wood and Stewart, aided by the women, to extinguish the flames, while he commanded at the loop-holes, and replied to the fire of the Indians, which soon ceased.

The fire extinguished, the dead body of Conrad Stiefel was brought down from the platform over the gate.

The Indians, under cover of night, had crept near enough to shoot poor Con, and fling fire into the loop-hole of a flanker, where were bundles of flax, straw, candlewood, corn-cobs, and other combustible materials.

"Children," said Blanchard, " mind what I say: don't fire till I give the word, and don't waste one kernel of powder nor one ounce of lead, for your powder's your life."

All through the forenoon the woods were as quiet as though there was not an enemy within a hundred miles; but this did not deceive Blanchard, who caused the drum to be beat, and gave orders to have imaginary soldiers, by putting clothes and hats on stakes, set on the platforms, in order to give the Indians the impression of a strong force in the fort.

A little past noon a band of Indians, more than forty in number, forty-three by Stewart's count, made their appearance, and, halting out of rifle-range at the edge of the forest, remained grouped together, evidently expecting some demonstration upon the part of the garrison; but no one mounted to the platform over the gate, the usual place for communication upon the part of the garrison. An Indian, laying aside his rifle, advanced a short distance before the rest, holding up his hand in token of his wish for a parley; but even of this no notice was taken.

He remained stationary a few moments, and then, advancing till he was within long rifle-range, again held up his hand.

The next instant the sharp report of a rifle was heard, and the savage fell dead in his tracks.

A fierce yell rose from the forest, followed by a shower of bullets.

" Don't fire," shouted Blanchard: " they are out of range, and will keep out of range, I reckon."

When the smoke cleared away, the Indians had vanished, taking the body of their companion with them.

" What made you shoot him, Blanchard, when he came to have a talk?" asked Holt.

" All he wanted was to tell us if we would surrender they would spare our lives, and then butcher us the moment they got inside the fort. If we had offered to talk, that would have been plain language to them, as much as to say, We know we can't hold out, and want to make terms; but when I shot that beggar down it was just saying, We neither love nor fear you : come on."

Unfortunately, however, Blanchard was mistaken in respect to the knowledge possessed by the enemy of the strength of the garrison.

Three scalping-parties of Delawares met each other on their return from the Susquehanna, and, after uniting their forces, had passed the Wolf Run settlement, not caring, though so numerous, to meddle with the settlers, being well acquainted with their fighting qualities, and most of whom they knew personally.

Encumbered with plunder and seven captives, two men, three women, and two boys, they were in full march for one of their haunts at Logstown, when, to their great joy, they struck the trail made by the party of Holdness on their way to Fort Cumberland.

They were not long in ascertaining the numbers of the band, and that the trail was recent; also, by the direction, divined the errand upon which they were going. The Indians forthwith killed and scalped their captives, secreted their plunder, and made their way to the neighborhood of the garrison, there struck the trail of the other party that had gone to Fort Allen, and counted the graves of the dead, and thus ascertained the weakness of the garrison.

Knowing by bitter experience the character of the men (few as they might be in numbers) with whom they had to deal, and fearing the return of the parties sent out, they had resorted to a parley as the readiest means of obtaining their object, but, foiled in this, resorted to bolder methods.

At daybreak the next morning the settlers were

greeted with a shower of bullets at close range, shot from a breastwork (within a few yards of the walls made) by the Indians during the night, from some timbers that had been negligently left while building the mill, and logs brought from Cuthbert's fences.

Some bullets entered the loop-holes; one chipped the stock of Stewart's rifle, and another wounded Wood slightly in the arm; and shortly after Maud Stewart, while bringing water to Tony and Sam, was shot in the neck, but the wound, though severe, was not mortal.

The children were now sent into the block-house, as it had become very dangerous to stand at the loop-holes, the Indians being near enough to fire into them frequently.

"If we should fire ane o' the muckle guns," said Stewart, "it wad make that same breastwork too hot for them."

"I'd do it," said Blanchard, "if I knew one discharge would drive 'em off; but it would take most all our powder to load, and, if they did not give it up, then we should be worse off than at present."

When the second stockade was built, it was

placed very near to the edge of the declivity upon which the garrison stood, and where the surplus waters of the spring that supplied the settlers found their way between the pickets.

The Indians, under cover of night, with some broken hoes that they found in the abandoned houses of the settlers, dug away the earth softened by the water of the spring, and the frosts of the previous winter, till but little labor was requisite to open a passage that would admit the entrance of a man. This they effected without the knowledge of the settlers.

When morning came they opened a heavy fire, filled the air with yells, and shot arrows to which they had bound torches of birch-bark against the mill. While the main body of them thus occupied the attention of the whites, a select band finished the excavation, and effected an entrance.

The war-whoop and a fire that, however, harmed no one, was the first notice Blanchard and his men received of their danger. Far otherwise was the effect of the fire returned by the settlers. Four out of eight of the enemy fell; and the rest had turned to flee, when the savages without, hearing the shout of their comrades placing timbers against the walls, and supported upon each other's shoulders, began to pour over the pickets, and opened the gate to those remaining behind, while those who were about to flee returned emboldened by the presence of their comrades.

Thus attacked from two directions, and their ammunition exhausted, the settlers sullenly retreated within the second stockade, with the exception of Uncle Seth, who, we are sorry to inform our readers, had taken no part in the defence of the garrison; but, soon after the attack began in the morning, had shut himself in the mill.

At the imminent risk of his own life, his brother lingered behind the rest, knocked on the door with the breech of his rifle, and begged him to come out and go with them; but he lacked the courage to leave his retreat, lacked courage to save himself.

Strange that those nursed at the same breast should so differ! that while Israel was insensible to fear, courting danger and exposure, Seth quaked at the sound of the war-whoop.

Elated with the advantage gained, the Indians proceeded in a manner and with a boldness quite

THE MILL WORKS WELL. Page 250.

in contrast with their usual cautious mode of warfare; for they had now discovered that their implacable foes were destitute of ammunition and well-nigh in their power.

In this enclosure, between the two stockades, was the mill, stacks of hay, heaps of brush, piles of firewood, and a great quantity of timber and chips which accumulated while the mill was building.

The Indians instantly resolved to burn the mill, thinking, that, as the wind was blowing directly from it to the fort, they might thus burn down all the defences of the settlers; and immediately began to surround the building with the combustibles ready to their hands.

On the other hand, the settlers were preparing water in large troughs to extinguish the flames, and the women heating some to pour upon the assailants, should they come to close quarters; also carrying stones and logs of wood to the roofs of the block-house and flankers, to fling down upon them.

All, even the children, were armed, and, expecting no mercy, had determined to sell their lives dearly. In the mean time Mr. Seth, from the loop-hole in the overhang, was witnessing the preparations of the savages to burn him alive. The poor man ran round the mill, wringing his hands, and a cold perspiration bathed his limbs. At one time he scanned the woods in hopes to see help coming, at another cried to God for mercy; while the Indians, who had discovered that there was a man in the mill, drowned his cries in shouts of triumph. Those vindictive foes had nearly completed their preparations. Several of them were on the top of the pile, taking and arranging the brush and hay; others were handing up to them; while a tall savage stood impatiently waving a fire brand, and waiting to kindle the heap.

At once a sharp creaking sound came from the head of the mill. The Indians paused in their efforts, and looked up in amazement. Israel Blanchard raised his rifle in which was the last charge of powder among them.

Mrs. Sumerford was on her knees praying, when the mill started.

Two of the Indians were within three feet of one of the vanes. The edge of the great arm in its descent lifted and flung one against the outer stockade, with a force that drove the breath from his body, scattering the wood, hay, and brush like the chaff of the summer threshing-floor.

The other, catching hold of the arm, was whirled high in air, stretched out like a string, and when the arm came down was flung with tremendous force over the picket into the garrison-yard, and into the very midst of his foes, but killed by the force of the fall.

With shrieks of terror the Indians fled.

The rifle of Blanchard cracked; and the savage who was the object of his aim fell just as he was running through the gate with the blazing torch in his hand.

Mr. Seth had lifted the brake, and let the mill loose.

The strange creaking heard was occasioned by the shrinking of the wedges that confined the arms, permitting them to work in the mortises of the shaft.

"We are saved," shouted Blanchard, "and that, too, by the only man in this Run that has no fight in him."

(Scip was not reckoned among the men.)

"O Israel!" exclaimed his wife, "our gratitude is due to a higher power than your brother Seth."

"I know that, wife, — indeed I do; but then Seth was a means, and a most strange one too."

"His ways are not our ways, husband!"

She received no reply; for her husband was at the mill-door, endeavoring to convince Mr. Seth that the Indians had gone, and that it was safe for him to come out.

"Shut the gate," cried Wood: "they may come back."

"And guard that hole in the picket," said Maccoy.

"Not they," replied Blanchard: "it's just their heathenish superstition. You'll not see one of those Indians again: they'll not stop night or day till they have put the Monongahela 'twixt them and us. They think the mill's a great medicine."

It was some time before Israel Blanchard could make his brother comprehend that the Indians were really gone; but at length he succeeded.

When Uncle Seth came out, the children hugged and kissed him; the marks of the tears still on their cheeks, which they had shed when they supposed he was to be burned before them; for, if there was anybody the children did love, it was Uncle Seth.

"We have been guilty of two great oversights," said Blanchard, " that people of our age, and experience of Indians, ought to be ashamed of, — letting that timber lay outside for the Indians to make use of, and using up so much powder and lead in hunting. If we had been provided with powder, not one of those Indians would have got over those pickets alive."

CHAPTER XIX.

THE BLACK RIFLE.

WHEN the boys and girls had finished their rejoicing over Uncle Seth, they bethought themselves of their colored friend; and " Where is Scip?" resounded on all sides.

"Dead, most likely," said Maccoy, — "scared to death."

After a long search he was found hid in the ground in a potato-hole, buried in earth except his head, and that covered with some rotten poles that had formed the covering of the pit. He was pulled out more dead than alive.

Notwithstanding the fearful position in which they had been placed, they left the garrison to occupy their own houses after the return of the two parties with plenty of ammunition; with the exception of Honeywood, who lived at the greatest distance. He moved into the house of his father-in-law, Israel Blanchard. Proctor, whose clearing was also distant from the fort, occupied the Cuthbert house. They attributed the advantages obtained by the Indians, to their own negligence in making too free use of their powder in hunting.

Scouts were sent into the woods; sowing and planting were performed by several working together, and the boys who were the least capable of labor were placed back to back upon stumps to keep watch; and one man remained in the fort to tend the gate, and fire the alarm-gun.

Our readers will recollect that the houses of the settlers were bullet-proof and loop-holed. The women were admonished to be watchful, and to blow the horn on the least alarm.

No one thought of making any improvement on his property. To raise food for themselves required constant labor and vigilance, and was only effected at the constant risk of life; for the whole country, from the Ohio to the Susquehanna, was swarming with savages, who often passed within sight of the forts, and insulted the garrisons.

The inhabitants of Wolf Run, however, bore their burdens cheerfully. They had both corn and wheat, and a mill to grind them. They acted upon the maxim, "Sufficient unto the day is the evil thereof," and rejoiced in flour biscuit, johnny-cake; and doughnuts.

One evening that closed a very sultry day, Maccoy and his family were sitting conversing with the door open. Suddenly they were startled by the report of a rifle; and, as Maccoy closed the door, he caught a glimpse of some one retiring, and a voice cried, "I have saved your lives." The next morning an Indian lay within a hundred yards of the door, with his scalp taken off to his ears.

"It was the Black Rifle," said McClure, when he saw the body.

The Black Rifle, or Captain Jack as he was sometimes called, we have referred to in a previous volume of these stories. He was one of those persons, not uncommon in those sad times, who, having suffered at the hands of the red men, had dedicated their lives to revenge. At times he associated with others, and commanded a company of rangers numbering some thirty or even fifty men, but in general chose to be alone.

As we have before observed, he offered, through

Col Croghan, to take his company, and act as scouts to Braddock's army; but, as they would not submit to the regular discipline of the army, the general would not accept their services; and to that refusal he probably owed his surprise and the defeat of his army.

The fear and the dread of him was universal among the Indians, who believed that he received supernatural assistance, or, as they termed it, was a " great medicine."

Many of the whites, amazed by the feats he performed, were of the same opinion.

He was partially insane, crazed with grief, lived by himself in the woods or in a cave, and associated with no one except for the purpose of killing Indians, and seldom entered into conversation.

Many a savage prowling around the homes of the settlers in the darkness of midnight, in order to shoot or tomahawk them when they came out in the morning, fell into the clutches of the Black Rifle.

The most skilful of hunters, all his furs were exchanged for powder, lead, and arms. The mission of his life, and which absorbed all his energies of body and mind, was the pursuit and destruction of the red man.

Though Honeywood did not live on his own place, by reason of its distance from the fort, yet he planted on it, and had a very large piece of corn planted on a burn. A large party of the settlers went with him to hoe it.

The Indians ambushed them on their return, but were discovered by Holdness. A conflict followed, in which the savages were worsted, and fled.

The settlers did not lose a man; but McClure was wounded in the thigh, and had to be carried from the field. Honeywood had his right arm broken, and Armstrong was hit on the left shoulder.

In this contest Nat Cuthbert manifested so much courage and skill in shooting as to receive much praise.

Five days after this encounter, Holdness was taken down with a rheumatic fever.

"God help us!" said Mrs. Blanchard: "here are all those most experienced in dealing with Indians, laid by in one way or another. What should we do if the Indians should attack us now? I don't know but we ought to go into garrison again."

In these circumstances Israel Blanchard expressed the common sentiment, when he said, —

"In that case we must fall back on Harry Sumerford."

Those model youngsters, Tony Stewart, Sam Sumerford, Ike Proctor, Jim Grant, and several others still younger, had been amusing themselves, by inciting and witnessing a combat between two bulls they had driven together, one belonging to Stewart, the other to Armstrong.

When the others had gone home, Tony and Sam resorted to the edge of a pond in Mrs. Sumerford's field, and procured some long sticks.

Getting down on their knees, they would creep along, and, running the stick through the grass, put the point of it under the belly of the frogs, who thinking it a snake would utter a little squeak, and leap for the water, to the intense delight of the boys.

While thus engaged Prudence Holdness came along, and wanted them to go down in the swale with her, and help get some herbs for her father's rheumatism.

The boys declining to leave their sport, she went on alone.

It was about nine o'clock in the morning, when Prudence started, leaving some dough mixed, that she was going to bake for dinner when she came back; her mother and Joan being occupied in attendance upon Holdness, who was suffering acutely.

Ten o'clock, eleven o'clock, came; and Mrs. Holdness began to say, —

"I wonder what does keep our Prudence."

By noon the fears of the mother were thoroughly aroused; and, not liking to say any thing to her husband, she put her shawl over her head, went to McClure's, and told him the circumstances.

"The Indians have got her: raise the neighbors!" was the startling reply.

Nat Cuthbert was well-nigh crazy.

"Harry," he exclaimed, "you must stick by me now. I'll follow her to Canada."

Harry Sumerford had not obtained the reputation he enjoyed, without deserving it. No less cool than sagacious and resolute, he said, —

"This cannot be kept from her father any longer: we must lay the matter before Mr. Holdness, and ask his advice;" and, taking Nat by the arm, he dragged him along.

When Holdness heard that his favorite daughter was captured by the Indians, and that Harry had found the trail, and the place where she was seized, he rose superior to his pain, and said, —

"Send Ned Armstrong here. — Ned, I believe you know whereabouts in the mountains Black Rifle has his camp when he's in these parts."

"Yes, sir: you pointed it out to me once. But I know him only by sight: I never spoke to him in my life."

"That's neither here nor there. Git right on the horses, you and Nat; ride all you know how for his place : I know he's there now. Tell him what's taken place ; and tell him that I, Brad Holdness, his old comrade, want him to take any of our young men he likes, and foller the trail. Give it all up ter him : don't pertend ter bother him with any advice, but tell him I'm laid by the heels, and trust altogether ter him.

"If you put it afore him right, and it strikes him right, and he goes inter it, he'll go inter it all over; and, if so be he does, there's no being, leavin' God Almighty out, can so help us at this pinch.

"Don't contradict him, nor rile him, for he's

notional, and may refuse at first; for he's not altogether right in his mind at times."

While Holdness was talking, Cal saddled the horses; and the moment he finished they were off at a spanking pace.

As they drew near the haunt of this singular being, Armstrong said, —

"Nat, we don't either of us know this man: who shall speak to him first?"

"I think you better, Ned."

"No, I think you'd better: you're the one most consarned. I came mostly on your account."

"But you've seen him; perhaps he knows you by sight; and you know what to say to begin with, because Mr. Holdness gave you a message. You know Mr. Holdness said we must not be discouraged if he said up and down he wouldn't help us, at the first goin' off."

"You speak first, and see what he'll say; and then I will."

They were now obliged to dismount, and ascend the steep side of a mountain, much of the way over steep rocks on their hands and knees.

"There he is," whispered Armstrong.

Beneath a projecting cliff, and by a fire at which

meat was broiling, sat the object of their quest, a man about forty years of age, of large frame, and exceedingly dark complexion, rendered more so by constant exposure to the elements, and clothed altogether in skins of different animals dressed with great skill.

He was evidently aware of their approach, and that they were white men; for his rifle lay across his knees, and as they drew near he placed it against the rock, and employed himself in stretching Indian scalps, several of which lay on the ground, upon hoops that were painted black instead of red, the color given them by the savages.

"That's what they call him the Black Rifle for," whispered Ned; "and you see he's got a black belt round him."

Resuming his employment, in which he had been interrupted by their approach, he took not the least notice of his visitors till greeted by Ned.

"Who are you?" he then said in a rough tone, "tramping the woods when the country's full of Indians on the war-path, from the Monongahela to Tulpehocken."

"We are Wolf Run boys, captain," replied Armstrong. "The Indians have carried off Prudence Holdness; Mr. Honeywood, McClure, and my father are wounded; and Mr. Holdness has sent us to tell you how he's down on his back with the rheumatism, can't move hand or foot, and he wants you to take some of our people, follow the trail, and, if they haven't murdered, try to rescue her."

"Can't do it, youngster. Sorry for Brad, right down sorry: him and I are old comrades; but you see it's just here. There was a family what I knowed, 'bout a mile this side of Gnadenhutten, not much more'n a mile from the fort (thought they were safe 'count of the fort), had a darter took sick, and died. They was buryin' her when the Indians come on 'em, killed and sculped her father and mother, two brothers, and four of the neighbors what was tendin' out at the buryin', and then took the corpse out of the coffin, and sculped that. There was thirteen of them 'ere Indians. I got word on it two days arter, and took their trail. There's the skin what growed on the heads of five on 'em [holding up the scalps stretched on hoops], and there's four more on the ground; and I lot to have the rest this moon. So you see how 'tis. Sorry for Brad:

s'pose your best men are disenabled [disabled]; but you must help yourselves, 'cause I took an oath, I'd have the blood of them 'ere Indians. Sorry for Brad, though."

"Oh, captain, don't send us back to Mr. Holdness with such a message! there he is lying on his bed in awful misery of body from the pain, and in distress of mind about his child in the hands of the Indians."

"Tell you, can't do it."

"If it was your case, wouldn't he do it for you?"

"Can't say he wouldn't: Brad and me are old 'quaintances. A better man never put a rifle to his face. But I must finish this business, 'cause a promise is a promise, and must be kept, 'specially a promise to revenge blood."

"Captain," said Nat, unable to contain himself longer, "that whole family are dead: killing the Indians won't bring them to life. But Prudence Holdness, we have reason to think, is alive, can be saved from a cruel death or captivity, and her father, who is your friend, spared the heart-break of her loss."

"Who be you that you set yourself up ter

chalk out for me what I shall or what I sha'n't do? What's this gal ter you, that you take so much on yourself? Do you know who you're talkin' to?"

Nat blushed, and was for a moment silent. "Captain," said Ned, "he is staying with Prudence, and engaged to be married to her."

"Oh, captain!" said Nat, emboldened now the matter was out, "if you had ever known what it was to have the woman you have loved from childhood, and hoped soon to make your wife, carried off by the Indians, you would not be angry, and would know how to feel for me."

Ignorant of the history of Black Rifle, Nat had all unwittingly touched a chord in the soul of this singular being, that roused and stung him to the verge of madness. His face flushed, his eyes flashed fire, his lips were drawn apart; and, flinging himself upon the ground, he tore up the earth with his hands. At length, having exhausted the intensity of his passion, he rose from the ground, and said in low hoarse tones, that as he proceeded became almost a scream, —

"If I had ever known! [repeating the words of Nat,] boy, you think you love that gal. I don't dispute it; and you think nobody was ever in trouble like you are. Just wait till you love a woman that much that there's nothing else in this world for you but her; you love the very air she breathes, and the ground she walks over; and you marry her; you make a home for the mother, the dutiful, trusting wife, and the dear little babes, When you return tired at night, the little ones come running to meet you: one takes your shot-pouch, one your powder-horn, and the littlest one runs toddlin' and screamin' inter your arms. One night you come home from huntin', and find only a heap of ashes. The Indians have been there. You rake open the pile, and find the bones of the mother, and the little ones all gone. When you've gone through that, you'll know something about the trouble that stings deep, and stings forever, and leaves your soul like stubble the fire's run over."

Here the voice of the Black Rifle failed, and his eyes that were bloodshot moistened. Tears were streaming down the cheeks both of Nat and Ned, when the former said, "Pardon my words if they have hurt your feelings: it was not on purpose. But oh, captain! as you loved those little ones, so Mr. Holdness loves his children; the Indians have killed two, and another is in their hands; and he, a sick, heart-broken man, sends to you. The last words he said to us were, 'There's not a being in the world, leaving out God Almighty, who can so help us at this pinch as the Black Rifle.''

" Did he? did Brad Holdness say that?"

" Yes, in my hearing," said Armstrong.

" Well, then, I'll go. Is Sumerford living at the Run now?"

"No, sir," replied Nat: "he was killed at Braddock's defeat."

" McClure, you say, is wounded: is Hugh Crawford there?"

" No, sir: he was killed by Indians not long since."

" Didn't Sumerford leave a long-legged boy, spry as an eel, and who takes to the woods like a duck to the water, and what's some with a rifle?"

" Yes, sir, — Harry Sumerford."

" Well, tell Harry as you call him, to choose two more, and meet me at sunrise to-morrow at the big sugar-tree that was struck by lightning three years ago, and stands in the clear in McClure's pasture. Now away with you: I want to be alone."

Without another word he entered a cave in the mountain, and closed a bark door behind him.

CHAPTER XX.

ON THE TRAIL.

GREAT was the joy of Holdness and his family and neighbors, when the boys announced the result of their mission.

"I shall embrace my child again," exclaimed the fond parent, speaking with difficulty between the twinges of pain.

"I trust so, husband, if the poor child is alive."

"I don't feel much afraid of their killing her."

"Why not? I'm sure they're bloodthirsty enough."

"That's true; but, like white people, when they're not in a passion they look out for their own interest. Captives just now are worth more ter them than scalps. A woman that's got a young child, or that's weakly, and can't travel, they'll knock on the head, and scalp, 'specially if they're afraid of bein' pursued; 'cause it's less trouble to carry the scalp than 'tis to git the captive along. But a good, rugged girl like Prudence, that kin travel right up, and has wit enough to know the consequence of laggin', they won't kill, 'cause the ransom's worth more'n the scalp, without they're like to be overtaken: then they will; but that we got to leave, and hope for the best."

Harry chose Ned Armstrong and Nat. The day was just breaking, and the outlines of the great tree were but indistinctly visible, as the boys reached the spot; but a fire was burning at its roots, and the tall form of the captain was seen by the blaze, cooking deer-meat.

"Morning," he growled, offering a share of the meat, of which he had cooked a bountiful supply.

"Thank you: we've broken our fast," said Harry.

"Then break it again, for you'll not have another chance in a hurry."

Harry and Ned ate heartily.

"Now for the trail," said the Black Rifle, much to the relief of Nat, who could not eat, and was in an agony of impatience.

Harry led the way down the hill to a swale

covered thinly with trees and a few bushes. The ground in this place was deeply imprinted with footsteps, and marks of several persons struggling. A basket filled with herbs lay on the ground, the handle broken, and trodden into the soil.

"There's the tracks of five or six Indians, and the track of the girl, for she was barefoot; and there's all the prints of her toes in one place, where the turf's off. I followed the trail a mile, most to the river, when night come on, and I had to give it up. Here's where the Indians made a blind with bushes, and when she came along jumped on her."

The Indians had cut some bushes, and stuck them in the soil, so they appeared to have grown there; and as Harry spoke he pulled up one of them.

Getting down on his knees, the captain examined the tracks with great attention, and measured several of them; in a few moments he pulled out of one of the tracks part of a side-comb.

"That was hers. I bought it of Simon Lombard, and gave it to her," said Nat.

Having finished his scrutiny, Black Rifle said, "That gal wasn't taken here; but there was six of them Indians: you was right about that. One's small; but there's one master big tall man, I know by his stride. I know the imp too: he's a Mohican, and has lost the great toe of his left foot. I've chased him afore."

"The girl wasn't taken from here!" exclaimed Harry: "when here's her own tracks and the tracks of the Indians, the basket full of herbs, her comb, and the blind the Indians made to shoot from."

"But the gal's tracks are going from here towards the stream; and she didn't fill her basket here nor back of here, 'cause there's none of that kind of herb grows here, nor 'twixt here and her father's; but she filled her basket somewhere else, and was coming back, or 'bout ready ter come, when they took her."

"Then how came that basket here?"

"The Indians brought it here; and the marks of a scuffle, the comb, and the bushes, are all their deviltry to mislead."

"I should think they would have known that somebody would think about the tracks going the other way, though I didn't have wit enough to."

"No doubt they did; but they were pressed

for time, knew they had only white men to deal with, and thought they wouldn't notice it. They wouldn't have tried that on other Indians."

They followed the trail to where a ledge rising quite abruptly from the low ground formed a part of a high rocky knoll of several acres in extent, while the trail continued on through the swale in a direction entirely different from that in which it had previously run.

The Black Rifle got down to the trail, and, after examining it a while, turned up a thin flat stone; and under it was a perfectly fair print of the girl's foot, but at right angles with the trail. He instantly ascended the knoll, guided by signs known only to himself, to a piece of very hard dry ground, to where a pine and hemlock had been torn up by the wind, the branches of which, as they lay upon each other, formed a dense covert.

"Here's where the gal was took. Here's where she filled her basket, and broke off the herbs: you kin see the stumps; and here," he said, holding up a plant, "'s one she pulled up by the roots and flung down agin, 'cause she didn't want the root.

"The Indians skulked behind them 'ere trees. There wasn't any scuffle: that big Indian would take her up like a baby. They took her down ter the rock. When she stepped off inter the soft ground, she stepped right across the back tracks; and they flung that stone ter hide it."

They now, returning to the ledge, followed the trail that was distinct to the river where was a ford.

"It's my judgment," said their leader, "that they crossed here, and kalkerlated by some of their stratagems ter cover their tracks on t'other side."

Crossing the stream, they struck the trail in the soft ground under the bank, but, as they came to rocks and firmer ground, lost it. Separating, they, for some time, sought without success to regain it.

At length the cry of the wild turkey (a signal agreed upon) was heard; and, following in the direction of the sound, they found the Black Rifle, who pointed to a hollow in the rocks filled with gravel and small pebbles, that had been laid bare by the subsiding of the stream.

"What is there?" said Nat. "I can't see any thing,—tracks or any thing else."

"Can't you see that these gravel-stones have been moved out of their bed?"

Taking one of them in his fingers, he returned it to the hole from which it had been dislodged.

"An Indian's moccason did that. Here at this rock's where they took ter the water."

"Perhaps the water did it," said Nat.

"I tell you 'twas done since the water fell, else the sides of the hole would have been washed, and the hole itself half filled up. Does the youngster think the water did this? [holding up a piece of red yarn.] This 'ere come out o' that gal's woollen gown when it dragged across that stump yonder. And we're on the right trail now."

Walking on the margin of the stream, they explored carefully its banks to ascertain, if possible, at what place the Indians had left the water; when Harry, who was foremost, suddenly paused beside a large, flat, white rock jutting into the stream, worn smooth by the action of the water when the river was high; and, after the delay of a moment, was passing on.

"What did you see?" asked Black Rifle, who was watching him.

"Nothing, only I thought that rock had curious seams in it."

"You thought right, for there's where they left the water."

This rock was striped with dull brown streaks running over its surface. The Black Rifle lifted his wet moccasons, and rubbed them off. Those stripes, mistaken by Harry for seams in the rock, were made by the muddy water that ran from the limbs of the Indians as they stepped upon it from the water.

Harry colored to the ears, but made no reply.

"Don't think twice about it, lad," said the captain with a delicacy not to be expected of him. "You're young yet, and haven't made trapping Indians the business of your life, as I have."

Passing over the rock to the bank, they struck the trail.

"The track of Prudence is not among them," said Nat.

"Yes, it is," said Harry, pointing with his finger. "That's it; but they've put moccasons on her. Don't you see that that track's smaller and lighter than the rest? There's less weight on the heels; and she toes out, while the Indians toe in. I've got the measure of her foot here on my ramrod."

Upon applying the measure, Nat was satisfied: not seeing the print of a naked foot, he thought the Indians had killed her. Though it was noonday, they stopped not to eat; but Black Rifle led the way at a pace that severely tasked the powers of the young men. If the trail was lost for a while on the hard spots, he regained it without the loss of a moment.

The limbs of his companions were bathed in perspiration, while his flesh was barely moistened; and he seemed insensible to fatigue. Harry, who had prided himself on his endurance, looked on him with astonishment, wondering what he was made of.

Just as the sun was dropping below the treetops, they entered upon a range of country which the fire had run over, killing the underbrush, and which was comparatively level.

"What a pity it's so late!" said Harry. "If we only had daylight before us, how fast we could follow the trail in this open level country!"

"No need of following their trail: they think they've done enough ter kiver their tracks, and don't try to hide them now, but are making straight for the old Indian runaway [path] that leads to their haunt at 'Turkey Foot.' But I kin strike that path by a shorter cut, and find it in the night, for there's a piece of a moon. They won't travel in the night; and so by the night travel and the short cut we'll more'n make up for the start they had of us."

As night came on, they drank from a brook, and took a lunch from their packs.

"Can't stop to make a fire," said their leader as he ate a little parched corn from a pouch at his belt. "A man don't want ter eat much if he's goin' ter make a push. When you feel hungry draw your belts tighter: 'twill strengthen the stomach, and do just as well as food."

Hour after hour till past midnight, this man of iron kept on without a moment's cessation, climbing windfalls, and dashing through brooks, until Nat became so exhausted as to run against trees, stagger, open long gaps between himself and the rest, and was just on the point of calling out that he could go no farther, when the captain, halting till the rest came up with him, said in a low tone, "I've got a shanty near here; but I must see that it hasn't been found and occupied by some redskin."

Giving his rifle to Harry, he entered the woods, while Nat flung himself on the leaves, and was asleep in a moment. In the course of half an hour he came back, and led the way to the camp.

It was built of turf and stones, in a little gap between two precipices, was covered with a roof of bark, and so concealed by shrubs and ferns that grew in the crevices of the cliffs, that there was very little probability of its being discovered.

It was entered by a hole just large enough to admit a man on his knees, the aperture being concealed by some spice-bushes growing before it, while the stones forming the sides and top of the entrance were so artfully laid, and covered with moss, that they seemed to form part of the original rock. Here, sheltered from the dew, they slept till break of day.

When Harry and his companions awoke, they found the restless Indian-killer had already made a fire in a hole that was dug in the ground in the middle of the hut, and lined with flat stones. He was broiling some dried deer's tongues on the coals, from which, and the provisions in their packs, they made a substantial meal.

Their host was not disposed to be communicative; but they gathered from appearances that the camp was a resort used by him while hunting; and that concealed in a cavity of the rock were not only traps and provisions, but·powder and lead, as he replenished their powder-horns and bullet-pouches before setting out.

The Black Rifle led the march for three hours, at the same rapid pace as before; when, stopping, he pointed to a tall pine standing upon a hill, and said, —

"Beyond that pine upon the hill is the Indian path."

With the greatest caution, as it was an Indian thoroughfare, they made their way to the path, that was deep worn by long use; and in a swampy spot found the trail so fresh that Black Rifle said,

"They are not far ahead. We have gained upon them latterly amazin'ly. They are kept back by the woman; and then they've not travelled nights."

With the same caution they returned to the place they had left, where they were concealed from the observation of any Indians who might be travelling the customary route.

CHAPTER XXI.

SURPRISE.

THEY had now ascertained several things of great importance to them: —
That the objects of their pursuit were before them, that the girl was uninjured and able to travel, and that they were fast gaining on the savages.

The Indian "runaway" wound round the hills and bogs, and was quite crooked; while the Black Rifle, leading them along by paths more direct known to him, was making a continual gain.

They pressed on with all the speed of which they were capable, and without breaking their fast, till past the middle of the afternoon, when, the direction in which they were going bringing them very near the trail, they stopped to look at it.

Their leader, after carefully examining the

tracks, next turned his attention to the bushes that in some places grew in dense clusters alongside the path. He said, after a long and careful scrutiny, —

"In my judgment it ain't more'n two hours since the Indians went along: the leaves of these bushes that they brushed forward haven't turned back as they were afore, yet."

While he was speaking, the report of a gun was heard not a great way off.

"They've been on the war-path," he continued, "eating only a little parched corn; and now they've shot some game or other, and kalkerlate ter have a fire ter-night when they camp, and eat. They'll stuff themselves, most like, and sleep sound. Then's our time to surprise them: sure as we come on 'em by daylight, and they see us, they'll drive a tomahawk inter that gal's head, and scalp her."

"Won't they do it if we surprise 'em in the night?" said Nat.

"No, 'cause they've got where they feel safe, and perhaps won't keep any watch; or, if they do, there won't be but one of 'em awake: the rest'll be scattered, sleepin' round a fire. We kin git 'twixt them and the gal, take kere of the watchman, raise the warwhoop, and what we don't kill'll run: in the dark they won't know how many there be of us."

"If there's risk of their killing her, we had better let 'em go; for even if they take her to Canada, or to one of their towns, she can be ransomed when the war is over."

"Let 'em go," said Black Rifle with a bitter smile. "That big Indian 'scaped me once: he don't agin. I don't take the back track till I have their scalps, or they have mine."

Nat said no more; and they went on, but more slowly, till the sun had set, when they once more approached the Indian path, and sat down to rest and eat.

The repast finished, they again set forward before the daylight was entirely gone, this time taking the Indian path till the Black Rifle stopped, saying he smelt smoke. Remaining a while on this spot, they again went slowly forward, till at a signal from their leader they stopped, and crept together beside a large rock that cast a dark shadow, and indulged for a couple of hours in the rest they so much needed, all sleeping soundly except their leader, whose restless nature would not admit of slumber, and who kept watch.

After waking them, he went forward alone to ascertain the position of their foes, and the chances for attack and surprise, while his companions awaited his return with feverish anxiety.

At the expiration of an hour, that seemed an age to Nat, he returned, and so silently that no one of them was aware of his approach till he appeared in their midst. To their eager inquiries he replied, —

" There's what I consider a right good chance ter git at and kill the beggars, part on 'em at least, and perhaps the whole. If we could all shoot, I should say we ought ter kill the whole; that is, 'lowin' we make no blunder in creepin' up, and if we could come in with four shots: but we can't, 'cause two on 'em are where we can't see ter fire, and must be tomahawked, and 'tain't likely there'll be a chance for a second fire."

" And you think there's a chance to rescue Prudence before they can hurt her?" said Nat.

" Yes, a good chance enough ter git the gal."

" Did you see her?'

" Reckon I did see where they've put her. The

gal, she's layin' on a little knoll; and they've bent down a saplin', and tied her feet ter that, and then they've bent another right acrost her, and fastened her hands ter that: she's right 'twixt two big trees. The large Indian's layin' on the top o' one of the saplin's, and another Indian on the top of t'other one, so she can't move ter speak of 'thout wakin' one on 'em.

"It's in the shadder; and there's a good chance ter crawl up behind the two big trees, tomahawk 'em both, and git 'twixt them and the rest, so's ter protect the gal."

"Where are the rest?" asked Harry.

"Well, you see they've built their fire right agin a big windfall, so 'twill most like burn more or less, the bigger part o' the night. Two of 'em are layin' side the fire, one one side, one t'other, their heads on a pile of brush agin the log; t'other two are afore the fire, one stretched out asleep, and t'other keepin' watch. Reckon that fire'll give light enough to shoot 'em by, 'cause whoever shoots'll be lookin' out of the dark inter the light, and 'twill give us a better chance ter see them than they'll have ter see us."

"The main thing, and what we are here for,"

said Nat, "is to rescue Prudence; and, rather than risk her life in the least, we must let the savages escape, and give up the attempt; for, even if they take her to Canada or to some of their villages, she can be ransomed."

"Reckon it's so with you; but it's a main thing with me ter kill the Indians. That big Indian escaped me once arter he'd been murderin' in the great cove; but he won't do it agin. His scalp 'll hang at my belt afore daybreak, or mine 'll hang at his'n: I didn't come ter make a botch of it. I tell you there's no risk of the gal."

Nat made no reply, but strove to quiet his anxieties, and hope for the best; for he perceived that the rescue and even life of the captive was of much less consequence, in the estimation of their leader, than the slaughter of the Indians.

Repose, enjoyment, social intercourse, and the kindly sympathies that bind men and society together, were to the latter words without meaning. Restless as the wind or the wave, he seemed constantly writhing under the pressure, or rather puncture, of one corroding desire, — that of vengeance. This fell purpose occupied his thoughts, and directed all his energies, leaving room for little else, and impregnated all his faculties. He indeed appeared, for the moment, to have been touched by the anguish of Holdness, and influenced to head the party by a transient revival of the affection that in other and better days he had cherished for his comrade; but it was equally evident that the bitterness of sorrow had dried the very sources of affection, rendering him in a great measure callous to the agony of others, and that, after all, the predominant motive that led him to join the young men was to secure their aid in the destruction of his foes.

It was now past midnight: the moon had gone down, and the dim light of stars from a sky slightly clouded scarcely penetrated the dense shades of the forest.

The voices of beasts and birds, that usually break the silence of a night in the wilderness, were hushed, and no breeze stirred the tree-tops.

So profound was the silence around the Indians' camp-fire, that the hard breathing of some of the sleepers, the occasional snapping of the fire, and the murmur of a distant brook, assumed an unwonted loudness. Stretched on the ground lay Prudence Holdness; and the dew of night fell cold upon her limbs, shielded only by the usual summer clothing she wore when captured.

From the moment of her capture she had cherished the hope that Nat and her friends would follow and rescue her, and night after night had lain expecting to hear the crack of the frontier rifle, and the shout of onset; but so much time had elapsed, and so far had her captors penetrated into wilds tenanted only by the red man, that hope had given way to despair. Stifled sobs rose from her breast; and big tears, restrained in the presence of her captors, rolled down her cheeks, that, fettered hand and foot, she could not wipe away.

The fire had gradually worked its way into the heart of the great tree against which it was built, blazing up brightly at times, as it reached some pine cone or knot saturated with pitch, rendering distinctly visible the grim form of the savage, who, seated before it, was holding his lonely vigil.

A form more fiercely wild, or better adapted to inspire terror, it would be difficult to imagine. He sat bolt upright before the fire, alternately in light and shadow, as the flame flashed up or died away. The blanket had fallen from his shoulders;

and the blaze that at intervals lighted up his visage, and played around his naked form, lent additional and startling effect to the terrors of the war-paint. He might have been taken for an image carved in stone, so rigid was his posture. At once, without the least noise, manifesting wonderful flexibility of limbs, he rose from his sitting posture. The body was bent slightly forward as in the act of attention; and his glances, that had been ranging over every object within the circle of vision, were now fastened upon the recumbent prisoner, and his hands grasped the rifle. With lips slightly parted, and dilating nostrils, he remained a few moments leaning upon his rifle, and then with his foot touched the slumbering savage beside him; but, before the latter could gain his feet, two rifles flashed in quick succession, and the half-risen savage fell back dead. The other, leaping forward with a fierce yell, stumbled to his knees, but, supporting himself by his hands, still strove to regain his feet when a thrust from the knife of Armstrong completed the work.

Roused by the firing, the two Indians beside the windfall, leaping up, strove to escape. The foremost disappeared in the darkness: the other, pierced by a bullet, fell back upon the hot embers; and the tall form of the Black Rifle was visible for a moment, as by the light of the fire he stripped the scalp from the head of the slain, and, leaping upon the tree-trunk, disappeared in pursuit of the fugitive.

Thus far no word had been spoken by the assailants; the report of rifles, and the sound of blows, mingled with the death-groans of the dying, were the chief tokens of their presence. But now the voice of Nat was heard shouting, "Harry, fling some brush on that fire." Harry caught up the pile of brush upon which one of the savages had slept, saying as he did so, —

"Don't shout any more: we are in an enemy's country, and there's been noise enough made already."

The brush flung on by Harry caused a bright blaze; and by the light thus afforded Nat was seen cutting with his tomahawk the saplings and withes that confined Prudence to the ground, and aiding her to rise.

Worn down with fatigue, terrified by the desperate conflict she had witnessed, and her limbs cramped by the pressure of the withes, the poor girl could scarcely stand; and, leaning upon the shoulder of Nat for support, burst into tears, but they were tears of joy.

That midnight scene in the lone forest presented singular contrasts. Here were the rescued captive, the enraptured lover, the rejoicing friends and rescuers; while almost at their feet lay the mangled bodies of the dead scalped to the ears, the work of Black Rifle, whose tomahawk cleft the head of the gigantic chief, while the other was slain by blows from the breech of Cuthbert's rifle; who, in his anxiety to rescue the object of his affections, had well-nigh disconcerted the whole plan of attack by prematurely alarming the Indian sentinel.

While Nat and Prudence were engaged in a whispered conversation with which we have no particular concern, Armstrong and Harry were busily occupied in extinguishing the fire, after which they sat down to wait for daybreak.

At the first approach of light they concealed the bodies of the slain under leaves and brush, obliterated all traces of the struggle by burning the ground over; and, taking the arms and ammunition of the dead, prepared to depart.

"Must we wait for the Black Rifle?" said Nat.

"No," replied Harry. "How can we wait for him? He'll not stop either to eat or sleep till he hunts down and scalps that Indian. He is alone, without fellows like us (that want to eat and sleep once in the while) to hinder and bother him."

"He's got neither home nor occupation, 'cept to kill Indians, and goes where his game is. He'll kill that Indian, then come back here, and scalp these we've hid in the leaves."

"I wish I could have thanked him for all he has done for me," said Prudence. "I'm sure I shall always be grateful to him, and so will all our folks."

"What a strange creature he is!" said Ned.

"I did but catch a glimpse of him as he stood in the light of the fire," said Prudence; "but I remember, when I was a small girl, of a man who looked so much like an Indian that I was afraid of him, and hid, coming to our house, and asking for tobacco; and how glad father was to see him, and how long he tried to get him to come into the house to eat and sleep, but no use."

"Father said he believed he had made some

kind of a vow, that he would not come into a house; and they called him the Black Rifle. I remember that."

"That was him," said Harry; "father never could get him into our house."

"When father found he wouldn't come in, he gave him all the tobacco he had, and this man gave him powder and bullets; father carried him out victuals, and they staid out and talked, and fired at a mark. The Black Rifle built a camp in the woods, and staid two days; and father staid with him."

"Then he liked your father," said Nat.

"Yes: father said they were soldiers together down in Nova Scotia, and that he used to be like other folks, and was a real kind-hearted man; but trouble had turned his brain; and that, of all the men he ever knew in his life, he never loved and pitied a man so much as he did the Black Rifle; and he'll love him more than ever after this, and I shall love him too. And to think I never had a chance to say as much as, I thank you!"

"He don't want any thanks," said Harry; "and he don't care any thing about us, now the

Indians are killed, and wouldn't be sociable, or have any thing to do with us. He'll come back here, and scalp them Indians; and then like as not he'll go clear to DuQuesne, prowl round there, and lay in wait for Indians; and the next thing you'll hear of him he'll be back in Anghwick."

"I should think the Indians would all get together, and kill him," said Nat.

"So should I," said Prudence.

"They would if they could, but lead won't kill him: a good many think he's something more'n a man. I make no doubt he'd 'a' killed every one of them Indians without us. He told me to take the powder and bullets, and divide 'em amongst us, but to leave the rifles in his camp; told me where to hide 'em, and where to find provision, and for us to help ourselves."

"What does he want of the rifles?" asked Ned.

"Sometimes he has a lot of men that go with him on a scalping-expedition; and some of 'em'll have nothing but shot-guns, and then he gives 'em the rifles what he takes from the Indians. Then, agin, there'll be folks, farmers that want arms to defend their families; and when he thinks they've pluck enough to use 'em, and not let the Indians kill 'em and get the guns, he'll supply 'em."

After rest and a hearty meal, they started, following their own trail, and travelling as fast as the strength of Prudence would permit, till they came to the camp of Black Rifle, reaching it just after midnight, where they remained all the next day.

They not only made use of the stores of the Black Rifle, but, finding in the camp a sheaf of Indian arrows, Harry made a bow, and killed two wild turkeys; and, being wearied, they spent the day in feasting, sleeping, and social chat.

By questioning Prudence respecting the place and manner of her capture, they found that Black Rifle had detected, with unerring sagacity, all the movements of the Indians.

"I used to think," said Harry, "that I knew something about following a blind trail; but since I've seen the Black Rifle I've altered that opinion. He's quick as a flash of lightning. He split that big Indian's head open, scalped him, shot another that was on the run, scalped him, and was off in pursuit of another, in three minutes."

"Why didn't you scream, Prudy," said Ned,

"when you felt the Indians' hands on you? If you had, some of us would have heard you, no farther off than you was; and we would have riddled them Indians with bullets afore they got to the river."

"I did try to scream; but the large one choked me so that I couldn't, and said if I made a noise he'd kill me, but if I kept still he wouldn't hurt me, and so I did; for I knew he could kill me before anybody could interfere."

"Could he talk English?"

"Yes, indeed, well enough. Why, Ned, that Indian has camped in the Run before the war, and, three years ago, came to grind his hatchet on our grindstone. I knew him the moment I laid eyes on him."

"Didn't you know we would be after you?" said Nat.

"I knew you would try; and I tried to drop something, or to leave some mark to guide you; but the Indians watched every motion I made, and prevented me. Once I broke the string, and let all my beads fall on the ground; but the Indians picked 'em up, and threatened to kill me; but the large Indian hindered them, and after that always kept me near himself."

"It's a mystery to me," said Harry, "how you stood it to travel so fast and far over rough grounds, and I suppose none too much to eat."

"No one knows what they can undergo till they are forced to. I knew if I didn't keep up the first part of the way, when they were afraid of being overtaken, they would kill me; and that part of 'em wanted to. All they had to eat themselves was a little parched corn; and my portion was small indeed. In the morning, when they started, my limbs were so stiff that I could only get on my knees at first, and after trying some time stand up. The last part of the way they shot a deer, and had plenty to eat, and went much slower; and that only made me think that they thought all danger of being overtaken was past; and that night, just afore you came, as I lay on the ground, I gave up all hope, wept, and asked God to have mercy upon and help me to endure captivity or death, if it was his will. When I had done that, I happened to look towards the fire, and saw the Indian that kept watch, listening and looking wild; and I listened, but could not hear the least sound. In another instant I saw Harry's face by the flash of the rifle.

It was as though I had seen the face of an angel; and the next moment I heard the sound of blows each side of me, and heard Nat call me by name. Then I knew I was rescued. Afore that it was like a dream."

At dusk they went on their way, travelling in the night, and concealing themselves in the woods in the daytime, following the Indian path so long as it led in the right direction, which afforded easier walking for Prudence. Their fare, however, was scanty, as they dared not shoot game.

CHAPTER XXII.

ANGUISH REPLACED BY RAPTURE.

THE denizens of Wolf Run were early risers; and, although the first rays of the sun were but just glancing on the lofty pines, the family of Holdness was astir.

Cal and Joan were milking before the door, Will Redmond cutting wood, and Mrs. Holdness getting breakfast. Holdness, though still suffering acute pain at intervals, was mending. At one time he was afflicted in his shoulders, at another in his knees and ankles,—a sure sign, according to Mrs. Sumerford, the oracle of the neighborhood in sickness, that the worst was over; she avowing that "a shifting pain was a going pain," an axiom not likely to be disputed. McClure was also able to walk with crutches. Every day he came to see Holdness, sat and rubbed his joints with a decoction of whiskey, wormwood, and comfrey-root.

During the friction Holdness would fall asleep, and, when he stopped, wake up in agony. However, he was now so much better that a good part of the time previously spent in rubbing and bathing was now devoted to smoking and conversation.

Mrs. Holdness, after getting her breakfast well along, entered the bedroom of her husband.

"Bradford, you slept more last night than you have at all: how do you find yourself this morning?"

"The pain ain't much jist now : what I have is in my shoulders and wrists. It's gone out o' my lower limbs; but my legs are so weak and stiff I couldn't lift one on 'em to save me. Ter think that a man who's been what I have, could be so whittled down, ter be no better'n a baby! I don't believe I shall ever be the man I was once : I'm all torn ter pieces; I haven't the strength of a green fly."

"Don't talk so, husband: there's always weakness after such terrible pain as you've, suffered so Mrs. Sumerford says. But Neighbor McClure'll come over by and by, and rub and bathe you; and you'll be able to sit up a little. We've killed a chicken. I'll make you some broth, and you'll feel better."

" I didn't sleep so much last night, wife, as you think I did; but it wasn't the pain of body altogether, 'twas thinking of our poor girl, that kept my eyes open.

" There ain't much time lost yet, because, if they've rescued her, she'll be worn out, and they must travel slow coming home; but, if we don't see or hear from her in the course of three days, we may make up our minds that she's murdered, gone ter Canada, or ter some Indian wigwam."

" If they rescue her, won't they send Harry, who you know can outrun most Indians, ahead, to let us know, and relieve our minds?"

" Don't think they would; for the woods are full of Indians, and they'll want all the strength they've got to defend themselves, for I don't expect Black Rifle'll come back with 'em."

" I thought, after you knew Black Rifle was going with them, you felt quite sure they would succeed."

" He will do all man can do; and, had he been on the ground the day she was carried away, there would be no doubt of it. But they had the bigger part of a day ter kiver their tracks, and ther 's a whole night besides ter travel; and that's a great start."

" You said at first they wouldn't kill her, 'cause the ransom would be worth more to them than the scalp-money."

"I know I did, and perhaps I ought ter feel that way still; but, as the time passes, doubts creep in, perhaps 'cause I'm weak and childish. I know they sometimes quarrel about prisoners: one claims them, and another claims them; then one will kill a prisoner to spite another; and then agin a chief'll kill a captive they're disputing about ter settle the matter, scalp him or her, and divide the bounty."

"Well, I'm going to try to be resigned, and to leave our child in the hands of a higher power. I find relief in so doing now, and if I never see her again I hope I shall find support likewise. Oh, husband, I wish you would do the same!"

"That may do for you, wife, and I s'pose you find comfort in it; fact, know you do. But I'm not that way inclined: there's no reality in it ter me."

" Husband, that's all the reality there is." The

smell of burning victuals called Mrs. Holdness to the kitchen, and interrupted the conversation. Cal, and Will Redmond, took Holdness from the bed, for it to be made, then placed him upon the side of it with his feet on a pillow laid on the floor; and he ate his breakfast.

Soon McClure came hobbling in.

" Good morning, Brad: glad to see you out of your nest. How do you find yourself? "

" Better: the pain's left my hips and lower limbs; and I think after you rub me I might bear a little weight on my legs."

" No tidings of the girl yet? "

" No, but I try ter think there ain't much time lost."

" I think no news's good news. They've had a great start, them Indians has, and I think it's all the better; for, sure as the sun rose this morning, Black Rifle'll overtake 'em, and they'll grow careless thinking they've got off; and he'll surprise 'em."

" I hope you're right: what are the neighbors about ter-day? "

" The neighbors are all gone or goin' in one squad to cut Honeywood's hay, 'cause it has the look of a right good hay-day; and his place's so far off they're goin' in force: part work on the hay, and part keep guard."

" Who's in the fort ? "

" Honeywood."

" Strong garrison: one man, and he with but one arm."

" He thought he could open the gate, and fire the gun with one hand in case of alarm, and that would leave one man more to work on the hay."

After a thorough rubbing by McClure, Holdness, with the assistance of his wife and Cal, managed to stand on his feet for a few moments, and to take several steps, but was so fatigued by the effort, as to be compelled to lie down; and had just obtained an easy position in bed, when the report of a gun was heard in the direction of the river.

" What does that mean ? " said Holdness. In a few minutes there was another, and not far away.

" That means Indians," said McClure. Before the words were well out of his mouth, the alarm-gun sent its summons over the hills.

" Father," said Cal, " I'll put the oxen on ter the sled, and haul you and Mr. McClure to the fort."

"The house is fort enough for us, my boy, — loop-holed, got an overhang, bullet-proof shutters, and will stand a good brush. 'Twill take more'n ten Indians, or twenty, to drive McClure and me out of it: we've rifles enough, ammunition enough, and I'm not goin ter leave it," said Holdness, his old energy restored by the presence of danger. "We kin hold out, at any rate, till they relieve us from the fort."

"Husband, you must be deranged. This morning you couldn't lift a finger to feed yourself: I had to put the victuals into your mouth; and now you talk about defending the house."

"Tell you it's all gone, every bit of it."

"The pain may have gone for a moment, but you have not a particle of strength: it is not three minutes since you tried to take three or four steps, and had to lie right down."

"Do, father," said Joan, "let Cal put some brush and a bed on the sled: I'll hold your head, and we'll take you to the fort."

"Sha'n't do it. Cal, do you and Will shove this bedstead up ter the loop-holes, so that McClure and I kin set on the edge of it, and fire out of the loop-holes."

" Father, you can't lift a rifle."

" Bring it here, and my bullet-pouch, and see; and bring, for McClure, that rifle I bought three years ago at Lancaster."

Cal brought the rifles, thinking that would decide the matter; when, to the utter astonishment of his family, Holdness took the rifle, and, putting the breech on the floor, loaded it nearly as quick as McClure did his.

McClure's wife now came in on her way to the garrison, and added her entreaties to those of Cal and his mother, to persuade the two cripples to seek safety in the garrison; but in vain.

" Brad and I are good for the lower part," said McClure: " there's plenty of powder and lead. Cal kin look out for the chamber, and fire down if they try to break the door. We kin stand a good smart siege till they relieve us from the fort. I never was much inclined ter run when I had legs ter run with."

Women and children were now seen hastening to the fort, all carrying the articles they most needed in their hands.

In a few minutes the boys who composed the company of the Screeching Catamounts, armed to the teeth with smooth-bores, knives, and tomahawks, commanded by Tony Stewart and Sam Sumerford, were seen bringing up the rear, keeping rank, and marching with all the composure of those who had more than once been under fire, heard the sound of the war-whoop, and knew that Holdness and McClure were looking at them.

The men had not yet arrived from the hayfield: that was some distance from the fort.

"What's the time of day, my lads?" shouted Holdness through the loop-hole. "Are your guns loaded?"

"Yes, sir," replied Tony. "Sam and I have got a bullet and three buckshot in ours."

"Cal," said his father, "go out and scout round, and see if you kin find out what it's all about: there may be nothin' in it, arter all. Some of the boys that are keepin' guard might see a bush move, and think 'twas the Indians, when 'twas only a critter rubbin' agin it."

"I don't like to leave you, father."

"Nonsense! I'm all right. Jest set me up a little straighter, and put some chairs or somethin' behind me ter block me up, and put the bedclothes 'twixt 'em and my back."

"Cal," said McClure, "afore you go, just put this lame leg of mine on a stool. We shouldn't amount to much, Brad, in a hand-to-hand tussle; but if an Indian comes in range he'll find we're some yet on a grooved barrel."

"I had sharp pain in my shoulders and all through me; but I don't feel one bit of it now."

"O husband! I'm afraid you'll pay for this: I wish you"—

Her voice was drowned in the shouts of Cal, who was thundering at the door with the breech of his rifle, and screaming, "They've come,— Prudy, Nat, and all of 'em: they're right here, I tell you, behind the woodpile. Oh!"

Half beside herself with joy, the mother unbarred the door, and rushed out, followed by Joan, and Will Redmond.

Another moment, and Holdness rushed by them looking more like a spectre than any thing else, pale as ashes, and his naturally gaunt form more attenuated by pain and sickness, and flinging his arms (that an hour before he could not move even to feed himself) around the neck of Prudence, cried, "My child, my child!" when, strength and voice failing together, he fainted, and would have fallen to the ground had he not been caught in the arms of Nat, and Harry Sumerford.

Israel Blanchard now arriving on horseback from the hayfield, with several others, they carried Holdness to the house, and put him into bed.

The clearing of Honeywood being the most distant from the fort of any of the settlers, they had taken their mules and horses to the hayfield; and Prudence and her rescuers were instantly surrounded by a crowd of women on their way to the fort, of men who had come on horseback, and the young men who were constantly arriving on the run, having outstripped their more elderly companions.

"What made you scare everybody to death? we thought 'twas the Indians," said McClure, coming up on his crutches.

"Hope you'll forgive us," said Harry; "but we never thought about that till we heard the alarm-gun, and saw the neighbors running: then we were sorry enough when 'twas too late."

"Never mind that," said Israel Blanchard. "God bless the whole of you! 'Tis a blessed day, and we could afford to be stirred up for sake of the sight our eyes have seen."

"Bless the Black Rifle!" said Ned, "for it's his work, the greater part."

"Yes, the whole of it," said Harry.

"Some of you young men jump on a horse, ride to the garrison, and tell the good news to Honeywood and the folks that are there and on the road," said Proctor.

Holdness soon revived under the influence of stimulants; and, after conversing a few minutes with his recovered daughter, fell into a sound sleep, from which he awoke weak indeed, but free from pain, and experienced no return of the disorder, but rapidly regained his usual strength. The crisis of the disease had passed; and the shock of the alarm, and the joy consequent upon the return of his daughter, completed the cure.

Honeywood was in the habit of preaching (as Holdness termed it) to the children and young men; that is, he often spoke to them when they were together, or when alone with individuals, in respect to the improvement of their school privileges, and in relation to religious matters, also in regard to trapping, shooting, and defending themselves if attacked in the woods by the Indians. But Holdness never made a speech, or went beyond a few pithy directions and words of praise.

Now, however, he departed from his usual practice; and one day, when Harry and Ned Armstrong were absent on the scout, he got the boys, large and small, together, to practise them in firing, and after it was over said to them, —

"Boys, you see by what's taken place lately, what a great thing 'tis ter know the woods, know all the short cuts, the lay of the land, ter be able ter find your way night or day, to follow a blind trail, lay an ambush, and shoot ter a hair's breadth. You see that gal of mine spreadin' out them 'ere clothes: she'd 'a' been in captivity now, or killed, if it hadn't been for the Black Rifle, God bless him! You kin see, too, how much pluck and a good character for shooting are worth to a boy what's comin' on. Now you know, when I sent ter the Black Rifle for help, all the boy he asked about was Harry Sumerford, and left him ter choose the other two; and what a great honor and advantage it was ter Harry ter have the Black Rifle pick him out for ter be with him on a trail, and larn of such a man!

"You needn't think 'cause you're boys you ain't taken notice of, 'cause you are; and I want you ter take notice of all you see them that have experience in the woods do, and never flinch from duty; for the meanest critter in the world's a coward, and the next meanest's a liar. There's Mr. Honeywood and the Black Rifle, and Neighbor McClure, and others I might mention, are known all through these Provinces, as men who can put a ball where they want ter, and the Indians know and fear 'em; while there's hundreds of others never'll be heard of, and never ought ter be.

"Then there's a great deal in the blood and in the bringin' up. It gives a boy a great start in life ter belong ter a good breed. Folks are apt ter take ter him, 'cause they think likely he's a chip of the old block.

"You may know that, 'cause the fust thing the Black Rifle said ter Ned and Nat, arter he made his mind ter go with 'em, was ter ask whether Mr. Sumerford and Crawford were living at the Run; and, when he found they were both dead, he asked right off if Sumerford didn't leave a boy behind him. See that! he knew Harry had fighting blood in his veins, and the raal millstone grit. I want you ter bear that in mind; and remember it's a shameful thing ter flinch from duty, and disgrace your parents and your bringin' up. I had two as good loving boys as ever a father was blessed with. You know what they were. It's a pleasure for me ter think of, and a pleasure ter speak about 'em, because they died doing their duty; and some day I hope ter bring their bones home, where their mother kin see their graves. But if they'd been cowards, run away, come safe home, and left their character behind 'em, as hundreds of Braddock's soldiers did that day, they'd 'a' been despised above ground, and I could never have held up my head amongst the neighbors arter that."

Holdness was interrupted by the arrival of Grant, Maccoy, and Alex. Sumerford. They had just finished their morning nap, having been out on the scout during the night, and, hearing the firing, came to see what was going on.

"Who made the best shot?" said Grant.

"Fred Stiefel 'mongst the little ones, and Elick Sumerford 'mongst the bigger ones," said Holdness. "Did you come across any Indian signs on your scout last night?"

"We went out, the sun two hours high, but didn't see nor hear the sign of an Indian; but we saw Black Rifle," said Alex.

" Saw the Black Rifle ? "

" Ay."

" Did you speak to him ? "

" Barely spoke him: he wouldn't stop, he was goin' awfully; he'd struck an Indian trail, was out of powder, and was goin' ter his place in the mountain ter git more."

" Then you didn't find out whether he killed that Indian."

" Had his scalp at his belt: I ran long side of him. He said that was a smart Indian: he chased him all that day, and jest afore night got near enough to fling a tomahawk into his head ; said the Indian seemed ter be master scared."

" Don't much wonder," said Grant, " with the Black Rifle at his heels."

" There, boys," said Holdness, " them Indians'll be missed; the rest'll sarch and find 'em, know Black Rifle scalped 'em, 'cause they know his work ; and see what a dread it'll strike among 'em. It'll be a good thing for us, 'cause they know he spends more time round here and at Anghwick than anywhere else ; and they'll be shy of comin' where he's like ter be.

" Perhaps if you do your best ter larn ter

shoot, and foller a trail, that next time he gits up a company ter go on a grand scout arter Indians, he'll give you an invite, and 'twould be the greatest honor in this world; and I might perhaps speak ter him if any of you should seem ter be suitable."

The next volume of this series — called FOREST GLEN; OR, THE MOHAWK'S FRIENDSHIP — will record the progress of a struggle upon the result of which the settlers had staked both property and life; will place the Indian character in a new light, and bring to view incidents that require not the aid of imagination to invest them with thrilling interest.

Books Suitable for School Libraries and Prizes.

LEE AND SHEPARD'S DOLLAR JUVENILES.
New Books and New Editions in Attractive Binding.

THE INVINCIBLE LIBRARY.
4 vols. Illustrated.

THE YOUNG INVINCIBLES. BATTLES AT HOME. IN THE WORLD. GOLDEN HAIR.

THE GALLANT DEEDS LIBRARY.
4 vols. Illustrated.

GREAT MEN AND GALLANT DEEDS. By W. H. G. Kingston.
YARNS OF AN OLD MARINER. By Mary Cowden Clarke.
SCHOOLBOY DAYS. By W. H. G. Kingston.
SANDHILLS OF JUTLAND. By Hans Andersen.

THE FRONTIER-CAMP SERIES.
4 vols. Illustrated.

TWELVE NIGHTS IN THE HUNTER'S CAMP. THE CABIN ON THE PRAIRIE.
PLANTING THE WILDERNESS. THE YOUNG PIONEERS.

THE FAMOUS BOY SERIES.
4 vols. Illustrated.

THE PATRIOT BOY, and how he became the Father of his Country; being a popular Life of George Washington.
THE BOBBIN BOY, and how Nat got his Learning.
THE BORDER BOY, and how he became the Pioneer of the Great West; being a popular Life of Daniel Boone.
THE PRINTER BOY, or how Ben Franklin made his Mark.

THE NATURAL-HISTORY SERIES.
By Mrs. R. Lee. Illustrated by Harrison Weir. 5 vols.

ANECDOTES OF ANIMALS. ANECDOTES OF BIRDS.
THE AFRICAN CRUSOES. THE AUSTRALIAN CRUSOES.
THE AUSTRALIAN WANDERERS.

THE LIFE-BOAT SERIES
Of Adventures. By W. H. G. Kingston and others. 5 vols. Illustrated.

DICK ONSLOW AMONG THE REDSKINS. THE YOUNG MIDDY.
THE LIFE-BOAT. ANTONY WAYMOUTH. THE CRUISE OF THE FROLIC.

CRUSOE LIBRARY.
6 vols. Illustrated.

ROBINSON CRUSOE. ARABIAN NIGHTS. ARCTIC CRUSOE.
YOUNG CRUSOE. PRAIRIE CRUSOE. WILLIS THE PILOT.

KATHIE STORIES FOR YOUNG PEOPLE.
By Miss Douglas, author of "In Trust." 6 vols. Illustrated.

IN THE RANKS. KATHIE'S THREE WISHES. KATHIE'S AUNT RUTH.
KATHIE'S SUMMER AT CEDARWOOD. KATHIE'S SOLDIERS.
KATHIE'S HARVEST DAYS.

YOUNG TRAIL-HUNTERS' SERIES.
3 vols. Illustrated.

THE YOUNG TRAIL-HUNTERS. CROSSING THE QUICKSANDS.
THE YOUNG SILVER SEEKERS.

Sold by all booksellers, and sent by mail, postpaid, on receipt of price.

LEE AND SHEPARD, Publishers, Boston.

Books Suitable for School Libraries and Prizes.

Lee and Shepard's Seventy-Five-Cent Juveniles.

Popular Juveniles in new Styles and new Dies. Any volume sold separately.

The Golden Proverb Series. By MRS. M. E. BRADLEY and MISS KATE J. NEELY. 6 vols. Illustrated.

Birds of a Feather.	A Wrong Confessed is Half Redressed.
Fine Feathers do not make Fine Birds.	One Good Turn Deserves Another.
Handsome is that Handsome Does.	Actions Speak Louder than Words.

The Golden Rule Stories. By MRS. S. B. C. SAMUELS. 6 vols. Illus.

The Golden Rule; or, Herbert.	The Burning Prairie; or, Johnstone's Farm.
The Shipwrecked Girl; or, Adele.	
Under the Sea; or, Erie.	The Smuggler's Cave; or, Ennisfellen.
Nettie's Trial.	

The Upside-Down Stories. By ROSA ABBOTT. 6 vols.

Jack of All Trades.	Upside Down.
Alexis the Runaway.	The Young Detective.
Tommy Hickup.	The Pinks and Blues.

The Salt-Water Dick Stories. By MAY MANNERING. 6 vols. Illus.

Climbing the Rope.	The Little Spaniard.
Billy Grimes's Favorite.	Salt-Water Dick.
Cruise of the Dashaway.	Little Maid of Oxbow.

The Charley and Eva Stories. By MISS L. C. THURSTON. 4 vols. Illustrated.

How Charley Roberts Became a Man.	Home in the West.
How Eva Roberts Gained her Education.	Children of Amity Court.

Lee and Shepard's Dollar-and-a-Quarter Juveniles.

Young Folks' Heroes of the Rebellion. By REV. P. C. HEADLEY. 6 vols. Illustrated.

Fight It Out on This Line. The Life and Deeds of Gen. U. S. Grant.	Old Salamander. The Life and Naval Career of Admiral David Glascoe Farragut.
Facing the Enemy. The Life and Military Career of Gen. William Tecumseh Sherman.	The Miner Boy and His Monitor. The Career and Achievements of John Ericsson, Engineer.
Fighting Phil. The Life and Military Career of Lieut.-Gen. Philip Henry Sheridan.	Old Stars. The Life and Military Career of Major-Gen. Ormsby MacKnight Mitchel.

Young Folks' Heroes of History. By GEORGE M. TOWLE. 6 vols.

Vasco da Gama. His Voyages and Adventures. Illustrated. 16mo.	Marco Polo. His Travels and Adventures. Illustrated.
Pizarro. His Adventures and Conquests. Illustrated.	Raleigh. His Voyages and Adventures.
Magellan; or, The First Voyage Round the World. Illustrated.	Drake, the Sea-King of Devon.

Sold by all booksellers, and sent by mail, postpaid, on receipt of price.

LEE AND SHEPARD, Publishers, Boston.

PUBLIC AND PARLOR READINGS AND SPEAKERS.

THE BEST SERIES PUBLISHED.

Selected and edited by Professor Lewis B. Monroe,
Founder of the Boston School of Oratory.

HUMOROUS READINGS. In prose and verse. For the use of schools, reading-clubs, public and parlor entertainments. Cloth. 12mo. $1.50.

"The book is readable from the first page to the last, and every article contained in it is worth more than the price of the volume." — *Providence Herald.*

MISCELLANEOUS READINGS. In prose and verse. 12mo. Cloth. $1.50.

"We trust this book may find its way into many schools, not to be used as a book for daily drill, but as affording the pupil occasionally an opportunity of leaving the old beaten track." — *Rhode-Island Schoolmaster.*

DIALOGUES AND DRAMAS. For the use of dramatic and reading clubs, and for public, social, and school entertainments. 12mo. Cloth. $1.50.

"If the acting of dramas such as are contained in this book could be introduced into private circles, there would be an inducement for the young to spend their evenings at home, instead of resorting to questionable public places." — *Nashua Gazette.*

YOUNG FOLKS' READINGS. For social and public entertainment. 12mo. Cloth. $1.50.

"Professor Monroe is one of the most successful teachers of elocution, as well as a very popular public reader. In this volume he has given an unusually fine selection for home and social reading, as well as for public entertainments." — *Boston Home Journal.*

☞ *Particularly adapted for school use.*

GEO. M. BAKER'S POPULAR READERS AND SPEAKERS.

THE READING CLUB, and Handy Speaker. Being selections in prose and poetry. Serious, humorous, pathetic, patriotic, and dramatic. In sixteen parts of fifty selections each. Cloth, 50 cents; paper, 15 cents each part.

THE POPULAR SPEAKER. Containing the selections published in the Reading Club, Nos. 13, 14, 15, and 16. Cloth. $1.00.

THE PREMIUM SPEAKER. Containing the selections published in the Reading Club, Nos. 9, 10, 11, and 12. 12mo. Cloth. $1.00.

THE PRIZE SPEAKER. Containing the selections published in the Reading Club, Nos. 5, 6, 7, and 8. 12mo. Cloth. $1.00.

THE HANDY SPEAKER. Combining the selections published in the Reading Club, Nos. 1, 2, 3, and 4. 16mo. Cloth. Over 400 pages. $1.00.

"Mr. Baker has acquired commendable fame for his rare skill in compiling from various authors selections suitable for many occasions. Boys will find within these pages just what will suit them for declamation, and girls will cull prizes from the contents for recitation. Teachers will find material for answers to oft-recurring demands for assistance in finding 'pieces' to learn; and the general reader will discover amusement for the passing hour, whether his mood be grave or gay." — *Providence Journal.*

Sold by all booksellers, and sent by mail, postpaid, on receipt of price.

LEE AND SHEPARD, Publishers, Boston.

CAPT. FARRAR'S GUIDE BOOKS.

FARRAR'S ILLUSTRATED GUIDE TO MOOSEHEAD LAKE AND THE NORTH MAINE WILDERNESS; also, the Katahdin Iron-Works and the Gulf, the Monson Ponds, Lake Onaway, Sebec Lake, etc.

A thorough and exhaustive guide to the sporting resorts of Northern Maine. The country around Greenville, and Moosehead and Sebec Lakes, Katahdin Iron-Works, the tours of the Kennebec, Penobscot, and St. John Rivers, Ascent of Katahdin, etc., are plainly treated. Contains the latest revised Game and Fish Laws of Maine, besides a large amount of other valuable information, and a large and correct Map of the northern half of Maine, comprising about all of the wild lands.

256 pages. 36 illustrations. Paper, 50 cts.; Cloth, $1.00.

FARRAR'S POCKET MAP OF MOOSEHEAD LAKE AND THE NORTH MAINE WILDERNESS. Printed on tough linen paper, and handsomely bound in cloth covers. Large size, 20 x 24 inches.

Every tourist, sportsman, hunter and lumberman should have one of these maps. It includes the headwaters of the Kennebec, Penobscot, and St. John Rivers, and their principal branches.

Price, 50 cts.

FARRAR'S ILLUSTRATED GUIDE TO THE ANDROSCOGGIN LAKES REGION, CONNECTICUT, PARMACHENEE, AND KENNEBAGO LAKES, AND THE HEADWATERS OF THE CONNECTICUT, MAGALLOWAY, AND ANDROSCOGGIN RIVERS, DIXVILLE NOTCH, GRAFTON NOTCH, AND ANDOVER, MAINE, AND VICINITY. With 100 Illustrations, and the best Map of the Lake Region ever made. Handsomely bound in illuminated paper covers.

Paper, 50 cts.; Cloth, $1.00.

FARRAR'S POCKET MAP OF THE RANGELEY AND RICHARDSON LAKE REGION, CONNECTICUT, PARMACHENEE, AND KENNEBAGO LAKES, AND THE HEADWATERS OF THE CONNECTICUT, ANDROSCOGGIN, SANDY, AND MAGALLOWAY RIVERS, DIXVILLE NOTCH, ANDOVER, AND VICINITY. Neatly folded, and bound in handsome cloth covers. Indispensable to the Sportsman and Tourist visiting the Lakes. Pronounced by competent judges to be the best and most correct map of this country ever made.

Price, 50 cts.

Sent by mail, postage paid, on receipt of price,
by

LEE AND SHEPARD, BOSTON.

www.ingramcontent.com/pod-product-compliance
Lightning Source LLC
Chambersburg PA
CBHW030015240426
43672CB00007B/956